INVEST
Your Way to
FINANCIAL
FREEDOM

Every owner of a physical copy of this edition of

INVEST
Your Way to
FINANCIAL
FREEDOM

can download the eBook for free direct from us at Harriman House, in a DRM-free format that can be read on any eReader, tablet or smartphone.

Simply head to:

**www.harriman-house.com/
Investwayfinancialfreedom**

to get your copy now.

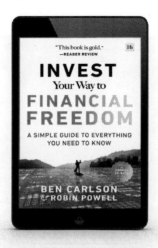

INVEST
Your Way to
FINANCIAL FREEDOM

A SIMPLE GUIDE TO EVERYTHING YOU NEED TO KNOW

BEN CARLSON
& ROBIN POWELL

Harriman House

HARRIMAN HOUSE LTD
3 Viceroy Court
Bedford Road
Petersfield
Hampshire
GU32 3LJ
GREAT BRITAIN
Tel: +44 (0)1730 233870

Email: enquiries@harriman-house.com
Website: harriman.house

First published in 2021.

Paperback ISBN: 978-0-85719-936-2
eBook ISBN: 978-0-85719-937-9

British Library Cataloguing in Publication Data
A CIP catalogue record for this book can be obtained from the British Library.

CONTENTS

INTRODUCTION: ARE YOU READY TO CLIMB A MOUNTAIN?

WE'RE NOT GOING to waste any time here. Let's cut straight to the chase: *most young people today are living under an illusion.*

This isn't a new phenomenon. Young people have always been susceptible to it and probably always will be. But, as we'll explain, it's an illusion that will have far more serious consequences for people in their 20s and early 30s today than it had for their parents or grandparents.

What, then, is the illusion we're referring to?

It's the illusion that money doesn't matter; that it's something only older people need to worry about; that things are bound to work out in the end; and that life's too short not to spend money in the here and now on whatever it is you want.

Don't get us wrong. Both of your authors may be long past the first flush of youth, but we've been there too. Youth should be embraced. It's one of the luxuries of being young that you can afford to dream, and to think about things other than work, money and responsibilities.

But dreams should be tempered with harsh reality. Money is important and it requires your focus *now*. Indeed, the earlier in life you focus on it, the less likely you are to worry about it in the years to come.

Marketing professor, author and blogger Scott Galloway sums it up like this:

> Successful people often unwittingly head-fake young people with the humblebrags of 'follow your passion' and 'don't think about money'. This is (mostly) bullshit. Achieving economic security requires hard work, talent, and a tremendous amount of focus on... money. Yes, some people's genius will be a tsunami that overwhelms a lack

of focus and discipline. Assume you are not that person.

This book is intended to encourage, inspire and empower you; not leave you feeling anxious. We're going to show you simple rules to set you on the path to financial freedom.

We define financial freedom as being able to live the life you want without having to work for money to someone else's timetable and without having to rely on luck, or others' generosity.

We're not going to pretend that any of this stuff is easy or that it doesn't require discipline and sacrifice. Young people today have a mountain to climb if they want to be as wealthy as their parents.

We'll start by explaining why.

THE BAD NEWS

In the great scheme of things, people born in Britain since the start of the 20th century have been, at least in a financial sense, extraordinarily fortunate. But some generations have been more fortunate than others.

Yes, there was the little matter of world wars, but assuming you survived those, the post-war years saw a steady improvement in living standards. Take Robin's family, for example. His grandparents enjoyed the comparative luxury of council housing, the new National Health Service and a fairly generous state pension. Those in the next generation – the so-called baby boomers – were even luckier, with most people owning their own home and foreign holidays becoming the norm.

Robin is from Generation X, which has arguably been the most fortunate of all. Not only did living standards keep on rising, but the state continued to provide a safety net, as well as free grants for school leavers to go to university.

Ben is one of the older members of Generation Y, often called millennials, and for that cohort, financial independence will be harder to achieve. It will be harder still for Generation Z – those born from the mid-to-late 1990s onwards.

So, what happened? Why were the baby boomers so much more secure financially than many of those entering the world of work today are ever likely to be?

Less generous pensions

Perhaps the most important factor is that pension provision for older generations was rather more substantial than it is today. Most workplace pension schemes in the past were defined benefit (DB) schemes; in other words, you were guaranteed to be paid an agreed percentage of your final salary, or your average career salary, in retirement.

Nowadays, however, almost all pensions are defined contribution (DC) schemes; in other words, the employee and employer agree to contribute a certain amount to the scheme, but the value of the pension pot goes up and down depending on how the underlying investments perform.

In short, DC schemes are much less generous than DB schemes. It's true that, as things stand, everyone with a total of 30 qualifying years of National Insurance contributions or credits is also entitled to a basic State Pension. But the State Pension is only a relatively small amount – £179.60 per week in 2021 – and there's no guarantee that there will even be a State Pension in the future.

Asset price boom

Another reason why young people face an uphill struggle financially is precisely the same reason why older generations have had it so good. Simply put, asset prices have boomed.

Houses, in particular, are far less affordable for first-time buyers today than they were for previous generations. In the 2010s alone, UK property prices rose by more than 40%, while most global stock markets doubled in value. Why? Largely because of Quantitative Easing – a policy adopted by central banks in response to the global financial crisis of 2007–9, to keep interest rates low and fuel the economy.

This boom in asset prices naturally benefited those invested in the property and stock markets, but it made both of those markets much more expensive for new, younger investors to buy into.

Slowing salary growth

A final reason why young people today are at a financial disadvantage compared to their parents and grandparents is that salaries, in real terms, have fallen in recent years.

A survey published by the Institute of Fiscal Studies in October 2019 found that "those born in the 1980s have income that is no higher in their early 30s than did those born ten years before – and this is the first time since (at least) the Second World War that that has happened."

Since then, of course, we have witnessed a global pandemic. A report by the Resolution Foundation published in March 2021 warned that, as a result of the coronavirus, many young people are at risk of pay "scarring" in the years ahead.

Traditionally, people tend to move jobs more frequently early in their careers, boosting their pay as a result. But, researchers found that annual pay growth for those aged 18–24 fell from 12% in 2019 to 6% in 2020. Among those aged 25–34, it fell from 5% to 1%. This deterioration in pay, the report warned, comes on top of the fact that younger workers are more likely to have been affected by furloughing and job losses.

The combined effect of less generous pensions, missing out on the asset price boom and stagnating wage growth has had a huge impact. Consequently, young people will probably need to make bigger sacrifices than previous generations to become financially independent.

But enough of the bad news. There are still plenty of reasons to be cheerful.

THE GOOD NEWS

Inheriting wealth

This certainly won't apply to everyone, but a saving grace for many millennials will come in the form of an inheritance. According to a survey by Hargreaves Lansdown in May 2020, young and middle-aged people are more likely than over-55s to expect a generous bequest. Around 22% of those aged 18–34 and 23% of those aged 35–54 said they expect a "large" inheritance.

A report by the Institute of Fiscal Studies in July 2020 claimed that a quarter of people born in the 1980s are set to inherit £300,000 or more, with one in ten in line to receive at least £530,000.

Remember, though, that nothing in life can be taken for granted. Nobody knows what the future holds, and it may be that a large chunk of your inheritance ends up being spent on medical or nursing care for either one or both of your parents. Bear in mind as well that they may live for a very long time, so you might not receive your inheritance until you are retired.

Saving more, spending less

Another silver lining, alongside this increase in inheritance, is that, contrary to the stereotypical view that most young people are reckless spendthrifts, the truth is very different. A survey by the Foreign & Colonial Investment Trust found that 68% of people aged 18–35 had plans to save more in 2021 than they did in 2020, with strategies including eating out less and cutting unnecessary spending such as takeaway coffees. Six out of ten millennials also said they would rather miss out on social occasions than borrow money.

Good time to invest

But there's a third and final reason why the pensions time bomb that many are predicting to explode in the middle of this century may not be quite as severe as it could be. In a nutshell, there's arguably never been a better time to be an investor.

We're not talking here about market timing. We have no idea whether stock markets are about to rise or fall. Nor are we saying that, in the next few decades, market returns are going to be any higher than they have been in the past; indeed, there is actually evidence that suggests they may be lower.

No, what we mean is that, thanks to new technology, it has never been easier to keep on top of your personal finances. There's a wide range of online services that allow you to set up a globally diversified investment portfolio in minutes. You can also automate your savings and investments so that the money leaves your account without you even having to think about it.

More important still, the cost of investing has never been lower. The industry has come under enormous pressure to reduce fees and charges in recent years and that pressure is intensifying. Most investors are still paying too much, but if you're smart about it, you can keep your total ongoing costs down to less than half of one per cent. Over many decades of investing, that will save you a fortune.

In short, then, previous generations have enjoyed significant financial advantages that millennials don't. But, on the flip side, young people can now invest far more easily, cheaply and efficiently than their parents or grandparents could at their age. This book is going to show you how.

YOU CAN'T BE TOO SCEPTICAL

Please read this book with a beginner's mind. Try to put aside any preconceived ideas you might have about money and investing; be open to the possibility that some of your views and opinions might be wrong and need to be changed.

Humans are very social animals. We pay close attention to what others are doing. When someone we know appears to have made a killing, perhaps on a property deal or on Bitcoin, the temptation is to try to replicate their success. But, chances are, your friend or colleague isn't an investment genius, but simply got lucky and bought at just the right time. You might decide to copy them and invest your own money at just the *wrong* time.

Wherever you look – newspapers, investment magazines, financial websites or social media – there are plenty of seemingly expert opinions about how to invest. The arguments are often perfectly plausible. But always exercise caution when someone appears to have the answers. Ask yourself:

Why are these "experts" saying what they are saying?

Are they really as smart as they seem?

Are they genuinely trying to help me, or do they have a commercial agenda?

Is the advice they are giving genuinely good advice?

Is what they are saying supported by data and evidence?

LEARN FROM THE BEST

Gurus are best avoided. There is, however, one investment expert we suggest you do pay attention to.

Warren Buffett is widely recognised as the most successful, and highly respected, investor in the world. Over the years, Buffett has passed on a wealth of knowledge and insight to investors, both in interviews and, in particular, in his annual letter to shareholders of his company, Berkshire Hathaway.

This book, largely speaking, is based on what Buffett has urged investors (young investors in particular) to do. We're going to be giving you plenty of practical details as the book unfolds, but as you read through the chapters, try to keep in mind these six fundamental principles.

1. Develop good habits

What's true of dieting is also true of investing: when starting out, it's best to focus less on the end goal than on developing good habits. "The biggest mistake," says Buffett, "is not learning the habit of saving properly." In particular, "Do not save what is left after spending; instead spend what is left after saving."

2. Think long term

Never mind get-rich-quick; work on getting rich slowly, which is far more realistic. As Buffett once colourfully explained, "No matter how great the talent or efforts, some things just take time. You can't produce a baby in one month by getting nine women pregnant."

3. Ignore market forecasts

Hand in hand with Buffett's long-term outlook goes his disdain for stock market forecasts. Nobody knows where markets are heading in the short term. "The only value of stock forecasters," he once declared, "is to make fortune tellers look good."

4. Be humble

Another important lesson that investors can learn from Warren Buffett is that they probably know less than they think they do. "What counts for most people in investing," he says, "is not how much they know, but rather how realistically they define what they don't know."

5. Keep it simple

"There seems to be some perverse human characteristic," says Buffett, "that likes to make easy things difficult." Successful investing is far more simple than many investment professionals make it look. As Buffett once put it, "You only have to do a very few things right, so long as you don't do too many things wrong."

6. Stay calm

The final, and perhaps the most crucial, lesson Warren Buffett teaches investors is to stay calm when others around you are overly anxious or excited. Don't be your own worst enemy. To use Buffett's own words, "The most important quality for an investor is temperament, not intellect."

YOU'RE ON YOUR OWN

To summarise, then, funding a comfortable standard of living for the rest of your life is a daunting challenge for those in their 20s and 30s. Don't kid yourself otherwise. That hefty inheritance you're banking on might never materialise; and let's face it, you're not going to win the jackpot on the lottery.

What choice do you have? People are living longer. Those in their 20s today can expect, on average, to live well into their 80s, and many will live beyond 100. Put off saving and investing now and you risk having to carry on working into your 70s. Worse still, imagine having to rely on the state, on charity or on friends and relatives to pay for your upkeep in your final years.

Ultimately, it's down to you. Providing for your future self is your responsibility and no one else's. But, if you focus on Buffett's six basic principles and take the steps we're going to recommend, financial freedom is perfectly achievable.

Let's get started.

CHAPTER 1.
WHY YOU NEED
TO SAVE

BROTHERS DICK AND Mac McDonald opened up a drive-in restaurant in the 1940s modelled after a hot dog stand they frequented in San Bernardino, CA.

By the late 1940s they decided to reorganise the business to take advantage of some lessons learned and the changing dynamics in America. The McDonald brothers recognised the burgeoning middle class following World War Two was moving to the suburbs and feeling more rushed than ever because of their commutes and growing families. People wanted their food faster, so the brothers mechanised the food prep process by turning their kitchen into an assembly line and focusing exclusively on burgers, fries and shakes. This was the invention of fast food and a little restaurant you may have heard of called McDonald's.

Ray Kroc was a milkshake machine salesman who saw potential in the business model, eventually manoeuvring his way into a job as the restaurant's franchise agent in 1954 to expand their reach. The McDonald brothers were not in the empire building business, but Kroc was, so he eventually bought them out and helped turn McDonald's into one of the most well-known brands on the planet.

Many years later, Kroc was asked why he partnered with and then bought out the McDonald brothers when he could have simply copied the system they created. Part of it was the fact that it was by far the best operation Kroc had ever seen of the thousands of kitchens he'd frequented over the years as an appliance salesman. But it was also the name itself that mattered. McDonald's sounded right to him, while a chain named Kroc's didn't have the same appeal.

The connotations we place on certain words can change how people feel about them, just like McDonald's versus Kroc's. The Big Mac rolls off the tongue a little easier than the Big Kroc.

Saving money is like the Kroc's of personal finance.

So many experts invoke terms like 'frugality' and 'delayed gratification' when explaining the merits of saving. Frugal is just another word for cheap and no one wants to be labelled a cheapskate. And delaying gratification sounds awful when you can simply take your gratification now.

Saving needs to hire a new advertising firm.

Here's how Don Draper might market the idea of saving money:

> It buys you time. Time is the most valuable resource on the planet and the only asset where there is no inequality. We all have a finite amount of time in any given day to work with. Saving money can give you more control over how you spend your time in the future. Time to spend doing what you love. Time with your family and friends. Time spent travelling to exciting destinations. Time not spent going to the office anymore.

Saving allows you to do what you want in the future without having to worry as much about the financial aspects of your decisions. Saving more now means replacing less of your current income when you finally become financially independent. A higher savings rate automatically means a lower spending rate. They go hand-in-hand. Saving is your front-row ticket to financial freedom.

Saving not only frees your time in the future but also gives you a buffer in the present. Saving money provides a margin of safety when life inevitably gets in the way of your best-laid plans. Life is stressful enough on its own, but adding financial problems can amplify the rough patches. The last thing you want to worry about when life throws you a curveball is money. Money issues amplify stressful situations.

The problem is most people don't dig deep enough when figuring out why they should save in the first place. Getting rich sounds like a reasonable answer, but living a rich life means different things to different people. A specific number doesn't make you rich. If you're constantly stressed out about money, it doesn't matter how much you have – you aren't rich if money still makes you worry.

Saving for life beyond work sounds impossible to some and too far off in the future for others. If you think about your savings in terms of buying units of time or freedom as opposed to units of money, it can help frame the decision into the proper context. Most people want to get rich but we would all be better off trying to not die poor, or better yet, defining what being rich means on our own terms.

Don't worry if you haven't got started yet. All it takes is some small wins to get the ball rolling.

CHAPTER 2.
THE POWER OF
SMALL WINS

A LOT OF ADVICE that comes from personal finance experts is borderline condescending.

Why don't you just spend less than you earn and save the difference?

Why don't you just stop buying lattes from Starbucks every day?

Do you know how much you could save if you just gave up your Netflix subscription?

Just put your money in the stock market and don't touch it. It's simple!

There is a reason most financial advice doesn't work: it makes people feel bad about themselves.

Financial advice sounds simple until you actually try it. Your finances can and should be simplified, but they are never easy because of the human element. There are so many choices to make that people can become overwhelmed. It's difficult to know where to start, which accounts to open, which investments make sense and what to do with your money when you finally make the decision to save. And for many, simply coming to that decision can be the hardest part of the process.

I'll start saving when I'm ready.

Save money!? In this economy!?

What's the point of saving money when the system is rigged against me?

Have you seen interest rates lately? What's the point?

It's understandable that people are often so overwhelmed that they ignore their finances or focus so intently on the minutiae that they never get started in the first place. But just getting started is the key because small wins can help you train your brain to see positive results that can be turned into lasting habits.

Take the example of swimmer Michael Phelps, the most decorated Olympian in history. When coach Bob Bowman began working with Phelps, they experimented with the idea of starting small to get him in the right mindset. Bowman told author Charles Duhigg:

> Eventually we figured out it was best to concentrate on these tiny moments of success and build them into mental triggers. We worked them into a routine. There's a series of things we do before every race that are designed to give Michael a sense of victory.

The idea is that giving yourself a sense of victory helps you see progress, which in turn sets in motion a compounding of other small wins that eventually turns into a routine that can make you successful, and this turns into big wins.

The same is true when you're just starting out as a saver. A team of researchers set out to help people save more money using the power of small wins. They discovered consumers were more likely to save when the decision was framed in terms of putting away £5 a day versus saving £150 a month. These numbers are basically identical, but more than four times as many people agreed to save £5 a day than those who promised to put away £150 a month.

How you frame these decisions can have just as big of an impact as the numbers used in your planning calculations. This same principle applies to paying off your debts. Once you get the ball rolling these things begin to snowball in your favour.

Let's talk from personal experience.

Ben's first job out of college paid $36,000 a year. After paying for rent, saving up for an engagement ring, paying back student loans and having a car payment for the first time in his life, there wasn't much room left in his budget for investing. The small firm he worked for didn't have a pension plan so after a year or so on the job he opened up a personal pension to begin his retirement savings journey. Since he couldn't afford much he put just $50 a month into a target date fund at one of the low-cost fund companies. It wasn't much money and it took a very long time to see results. But he took pride in the fact that he even opened up the account and soon it began to grow.

Over time as he made more money he slowly increased the amount saved. Every time he received a pay rise he would bump up his savings rate to avoid lifestyle creep and help juice his savings. It took many years to get his savings rate to where he wanted it to be. Making a higher income over time certainly helped, but the best thing he ever did to build good financial habits was just getting started. Those initial small wins set the tone to get where he eventually wanted to be in terms of saving because it helped develop the right habits.

The self-improvement writer James Clear shows the power of minor improvements in his book *Atomic Habits*:

> The difference a tiny improvement can make over time is astounding. Here's how the maths works out: if you can get 1% better each day for one year, you'll end up 37 times better by the time you're done. Conversely, if you get 1% worse each day for one year, you'll decline nearly down to zero. What starts as a small win or a minor setback accumulates into something much more.

Getting just 1% better a day would make you 37 times better over the course of the year. This is easier said than done, but it shows how tiny improvements can have big results over time. No one starts out training for a marathon by running 26.2 miles on day one. The same is true for your savings.

Let's say you start out saving 3% of your income with a goal of steadily increasing that rate in the future. If you go from saving 3% of your income in year one to 4% in the next, that's a 33% increase in your savings rate. Go from 4% to 5% and you've given yourself a 25% annual jump in savings. Getting to 6% from 5% is a 20% jump.

The goal when you're just getting started is to see an increase in your savings rate each year that is bigger than the historical return on the stock market (which has averaged 8% to 10% returns over the past 90 years or so) until you reach your steady state savings rate. (We'll explain this in more detail in Chapter 5.)

For example, let's say you are aged 25, you earn £40,000 a year and your monthly take home pay is around £2,400. You save 12% of that take home: £288. In the next year, you want to increase your savings rate by more than the historic return on the stock market (which has been 8% to 10%). A 20% increase in your 12% savings rate means you will now save 15% of your take home salary each month. You now save £360 per month (15% of £2,400).

It's also important to start building good habits when you're young to lessen the sting of saving more when you're older. Psychologists have determined losses sting twice as bad as gains feel good. If you wait to start saving until you're older, it will feel like lost income if those savings habits haven't been developed yet. Therefore, saving money will make you feel twice as bad later in life because it will feel like you're giving yourself a reduction in income.

Early on in your financial lifecycle, the vast majority of your gains will come not from your investing prowess but from your savings rate.

The next chapter will show you why.

CHAPTER 3.
WHEN SHOULD YOU
START SAVING?

FIRST THINGS FIRST: before you start investing, look at your debts. The interest you pay on debts is normally much higher than the interest earned on savings, so it's usually best to pay off credit cards, store cards or loans before you start putting money away.

Once your debts are cleared, prioritise building up an emergency fund saved in cash. Nobody knows what the future holds, so make sure you're prepared for a stroke of misfortune – losing your job, for example. Ideally, over time, you should build up your cash savings to cover six months of essential outgoings. In practice, though, covering three months of outgoings is probably sufficient.

You have to be able to take your money out as soon as you need it, so put it in an instant access account. The interest you earn will be lower than on, say, a 90-day notice account, but remember, this is an emergency fund and you need the flexibility.

OK, so you've paid off your debts and you have some cash to draw on in an emergency. You're now ready to invest in the stock market. And don't delay, because the sooner you start the better. Why? Because the longer you invest for, the more you benefit from what's been described as the miracle of compounding.

Take Warren Buffett, for example. Buffett is one of the richest people in the world and one of the greatest investors of the modern era, and he bought his first stocks at the age of 11.

On his 60th birthday in 1990, Buffett's net worth was close to $4 billion, according to the Forbes 400 list. By the time he turned 90 in 2020, Buffett's net worth had skyrocketed to more than $70 billion (and that's after he gave away tens of billions to charity). That means nearly 95% of Buffett's net worth was created after his 60th birthday.

We'll come back to this after we go through a simple example.

Most investment calculators offer you fairly simple inputs. You enter the amount you currently have saved, your future saving projections and a return assumption. Then the calculator spits out a future value based on those assumed inputs.

This isn't a perfect way to determine exactly how much money you will have saved up by retirement because life doesn't work in a straight line. Investment calculators are clean while the real world is messy.

Planning for long-term investment growth is more about accuracy (the ballpark) than precision (the bullseye), but running the numbers can at least give you a general idea of how your savings habits can impact your ability to generate long-term wealth.

With that in mind, here are some basic assumptions for a hypothetical young person with a long time horizon ahead of them that you might see in a typical retirement calculator.

Let's say you begin saving at age 25 with a target retirement age of 65. You start saving 12% of your annual income of £40,000 and your income grows by 3% a year.

So how much would our hypothetical investment calculator saver end up with in this situation? Starting at this early age of 25 and with a high savings rate would net more than £1.5 million by the time you retire at age 65.

Starting Age	25
Retirement Age	65
Annual Returns	7%
Annual Raise	3%
Starting Salary	£40,000
% of Income Saved	12%
Total Saved	£377,584
Ending Balance	£1,524,564
% from Saving	25%
% from Investing	75%

You can see that a steady diet of a double-digit savings rate coupled with decent investment returns and a healthy dose of compound interest can turn our hypothetical saver into a millionaire by the time they retire.

Looking at these numbers would lead you to believe that your investment returns carry the bulk of the load and that investment returns are the thing young investors should focus on, because three-quarters of our saver's ending balance comes from compounded investment gains. But breaking out these results by different periods tells us a much different story.

Here's how things look by age 35 if you were to start saving at 25:

Age	35
Balance	£87,135
% from Saving	71%
% from Investing	29%

As you can see, in the early years, the amount of money you put into your retirement account drives the bulk of your ending balance. It is saving, not investment returns, that is driving you forward.

Now here are the results by age 45:

Age	45
Balance	£274,932
% from Saving	50%
% from Investing	50%

It took more than 20 years for the investment gains to catch up with savings in terms of the contribution to the overall balance.

Here's a little secret about the compound interest that you cannot see in a retirement calculator – the majority of the growth comes once you build up a large enough balance as you get closer to retirement age. You can see this in action from the change in value over the final ten years of saving and investing:

Balance at age 56	£739,559
Balance at age 65	£1,524,564

The gains from investing in the last ten years in this example (age 56 to age 65) amount to £660,000, which is more than 40% of the total ending balance.

This is where the Buffett example from the above comes into play. Obviously, it's a bit of an unfair comparison because the Oracle of Omaha is one of the richest people on the planet. But both Buffett's growth in assets and our calculator example show how your money grows slowly until it builds upon itself and then explodes higher as compound interest takes off.

Real wealth for normal retirement savers comes from a combination of saving, compounding and sitting on your hands. No, not investment returns. Saving, compounding and sitting on your hands.

It takes time and it's not easy. It could take decades to see extraordinary results, which is much longer than most people would prefer. Saving is more important than investing, but saving is boring while investing is sexy.

A few more lessons from this basic example:

- It's more exciting to focus on milking a few extra percentage points of investment returns out of the financial markets, but the amount you save in the first few decades of your career is far more important than your investment strategy. As life expectancy continues to increase, the virtue of patience and an understanding of your time horizon become more important than ever.

- Increasing the savings rate on your income in this example from 12% to 15% has nearly the same effect on the ending balance as increasing investment performance by 1% per year. A savings rate of 20% instead of 12% equates to more than 2% a year in market returns. Earning higher returns on your investments is much more difficult than saving more money. You actually control your savings rate while no one controls what happens in the markets.

- Deconstructing compound interest into different time frames can help illustrate the power of sticking with a long-term saving and investment plan. It may seem like every tick in the market is going to make or break your portfolio, when in reality the simple act of saving more money over the long run can have an enormous impact on the size of your wealth.

- One study found nearly three-quarters of long-term investment success can be attributed to an individual's savings rate while the rest was explained by asset allocation and investment selections. For the majority of the population, saving is more important than investing.

It doesn't matter if you're the second coming of Warren Buffett if you don't save money. It takes money to compound money. Saving always comes before investing. But why should you save with the intent of investing in the first place?

The next chapter tackles this question.

CHAPTER 4.
WHY INVEST IN
THE FIRST PLACE?

T HE PRICE OF a cinema tickct in 1970 was around
30 pence. Today it's around £7.50. That's a rise of
more than 2,400% over 50 years. The average price of
a new car in 1970 was £1,000, while the price of a litre
of petrol was seven pence. Half a century later those
averages were around £23,000 for a car and £1.25
for a litre of petrol – increases of 2,010% and 1,685%
respectively.

Saving is more important than investing when it comes
to getting started with your finances. But if you ever
hope to increase your standard of living, you have to
grow your money over and above the rate of inflation.

If you were to bury your money in your garden, it would take just 23 years to see the value of your savings cut in half from a 3% annual inflation rate. At 4%, the half-life of your money would be just 17 years.

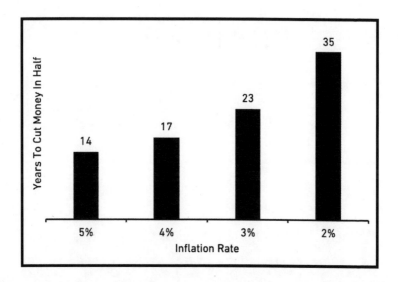

If you don't put your long-term savings into productive financial assets, your money is going to lose its value. Let's look at one of the most popular shoe brands of all time to see why this is the case.

After being selected third overall by the Chicago Bulls in the 1984 NBA Draft, Michael Jordan was signed to a five-year deal with Nike that was worth a reported $2.5 million, a hefty price tag at the time. A year later,

Nike gave Jordan his own signature shoe. The Air Jordan was born.

The rest is history as Jordan went on to win six NBA titles, numerous MVP awards and become widely regarded as the best player to ever lace them up. There have since been over 30 different signature Air Jordans in hundreds of different variations. Jordan's brand is so successful that he's now made far more money through his partnership with Nike than he ever made playing in the NBA. In 2019, the Jordan brand alone brought in more than $3 billion in revenue for Nike. That was good enough for roughly one-third of the total revenue for the entire company.

The first pair sold for $65, which was by far the most expensive basketball shoe on the market at the time. These shoes now regularly sell for $200 or more a pair, while certain models can fetch thousands of dollars. It's now been well over 30 years since the first pair of Air Jordans hit the market.

So, what would have happened had you taken that $65 investment in a pair of Jordans back in 1985 and matched it with a $65 investment in Nike (NKE) stock?

The price of a pair of Air Jordans grew from $65 in 1985 to $235 in 2019. That's an annual growth rate of 4% per year, outpacing the inflation rate of 2.5%

over that time. But Nike's stock appreciated at a rate of more than 21% per year from 1985–2019. Had you invested $65 in the company in 1985, it would have been worth more than $36,000 by the end of 2019. That's an expensive pair of shoes.

This is an extreme example using one of the most successful companies in history, but it illustrates the power of stock ownership over the long term and the need to invest in productive assets. The cost of stuff – houses, cars, food, clothing, etc. – generally goes up over time so you need to invest your money to protect your savings from the effects of inflation.

Time is your biggest enemy when it comes to the impact of inflation on your wealth. But time is also your biggest asset when it comes to growing your wealth.

A story about two different savers in the next chapter illustrates the importance of time as your biggest asset.

CHAPTER 5.
YOUR BIGGEST
ASSET

L ET'S BE HONEST – you probably can't spot the next Nike-like winner in the stock market and nor can we. Here's a more realistic look at how even modest returns in the markets can lead to powerful results, if you start early.

Sarah and Jon took two different paths on their retirement journey. Sarah was always a planner, so she made a point of saving once she found her first real job out of school. Jon, on the other hand, opted out of saving right off the bat because he wanted to wait until he was ready later in life.

Sarah began saving for retirement at age 25, setting aside £500 a month in her workplace retirement account until age 35. At this point, she stopped saving and let compound interest work in her favour. At age 65, assuming a 7% annual rate of return, she would retire with approximately £720,000, even though she only contributed a total of £66,000 to her account.

Jon put off investing for years because he always assumed the stock market operated like a casino where the house always wins. Once he saw Sarah slowly building her wealth, he finally decided to start saving at age 40. He followed her lead, saving the same £500 a month that Sarah did, but he actually does so until the day he retires at age 65. The total amount Jon contributed to his retirement account over those two-plus decades would add up to £156,000. Assuming he also earns an annual return of 7% on his funds he will end up with around £412,000 when he retires.

Even though Jon contributed two-and-a-half times as much money and saved for two-and-a-half as many years as Sarah, he ended up with £308,000 less than her at retirement.

How could this be, you ask?

	Sarah	Jon
Started Saving	Age 25	Age 40
Stopped Saving	Age 35	Age 65
Total Saved	£66,000	£156,000
Ending Balance	£720,000	£412,000

Assumptions: Each saves £500 a month and earns 7% on their investments.

Sarah made better use of her biggest asset – time – than Jon did. Her savings compounded for a decade and a half longer, thus giving her money more time to snowball.

This is a simple example, but let's not let Sarah off the hook that easily. There's no need to stop saving at age 35 just to prove a point about compound interest. Let's assume she doesn't stop saving at 35 but instead continues to dutifully sock away money each year until she reaches retirement age. Using these same inputs, she would now grow her portfolio to nearly £1.3 million by age 65. While Sarah would have saved £90,000 more in retirement contributions than Jon, she would have ended up with nearly £700,000 more by retirement age because she got an early start on saving.

The best thing you can do as a young person is to start saving and investing as soon as possible to take advantage of your long time horizon. According to financial writer William Bernstein:

> Each dollar you do not save at 25 will mean two inflation-adjusted dollars that you will need to save if you start at age 35, four if you begin at 45, and eight if you start at 55. In practice, if you lack substantial savings at 45, you are in serious trouble. Since a 25-year-old should be saving at least 10 percent of his or her salary, this means that a 45-year-old will need to save nearly half of his or her salary.

Starting at a young age not only helps you take advantage of compound interest, it can save you stress and financial strain later in life.

All is not lost if you're older and don't have access to a time machine, but it will take some more planning and a higher savings rate. (We're going to look at ways to overcome a late start to investing in Chapter 20.)

We used £500 in this example because it's a neat, round number. But working out how much you need to save is one of the hardest questions to answer no matter where you are in relation to retirement age.

How much you should save is up next.

CHAPTER 6.
HOW MUCH SHOULD
YOU SAVE?

O FFERING FINANCIAL ADVICE is always tricky because so much of it is circumstantial. It's impossible to offer investment guidance if you don't know someone's goals, needs, desires, temperament, personality and current financial situation.

In lieu of knowing every reader's specific personal and financial circumstances, a useful rule of thumb is that your savings rate should be in the double digits as a percentage of your income.

If you do nothing else in your financial life than setting a high savings rate you'll be alright. Ten per cent is a nice goal while 15% to 20% of your income would be even better. Can everyone afford to have a double-digit savings rate right off the bat? Of course not! But it's a goal you should work up to if you wish to create a large enough nest egg to reach financial independence someday.

There are numerous benefits that accrue from introducing a double-digit savings rate in your life:

- It gives you a margin of safety when life interferes with your plans.

- It means you have less income to replace once you become financially independent.

- It reduces the many stresses that come as a result of money decisions.

- How much you spend is one of the few areas in life you have control over.

There are a few ways in which you can supercharge your savings to get to a double-digit savings rate over time even if it's not possible for you right away.

TREAT IT LIKE A BILL

We have a finite amount of willpower, so trying to make it through your monthly budget and save whatever is left over will eventually become a losing strategy. You have to make your savings automatic so you can't tinker with that decision. Look at saving money like a monthly bill or subscription, like paying for Netflix or a gym membership.

Setting up a direct debit on your personal pension or a Stocks and Shares ISA makes this easy and convenient because you can set this up to leave your bank account soon after your salary is paid in, just like any other bill. Because you never see the money in your bank, in theory you shouldn't miss it.

Once your saving is taken care of at the start of the month, you don't need permission to spend elsewhere. You can spend money guilt-free without worry because your savings goals are taken care of. This is a way to think about budgeting in reverse.

Saving money should be prioritised every month just like rent/mortgage, utilities, internet, streaming services and any other regular payments. The goal is to save enough money out of each paycheck that it hurts just a little bit.

WORK YOUR WAY UP TO IT

Let's assume you want to start small because the prospect of saving lots of money from your paycheck is terrifying. If you save £100 a month towards retirement and your income is £60,000 a year, that's a savings rate of 2%. To get to our double-digit savings rate goal we have some work to do. Just a 1% increase in your savings rate every year could add hundreds of thousands of pounds to your portfolio over time.

Let's look at Karen as an example. Karen is 30 years old and makes sixty grand a year, saving £100 a month. If she were to simply keep saving 2% of her income (which grows at 3% per year for cost of living increases) every year until retiring at age 65, she would amass just shy of £260,000, assuming a 7% annual return on her investments.

Now let's see what happens if Karen were to increase her savings rate by just 1% per year. To hit a 15% savings rate goal it would take 14 years, which sounds like forever. But this allows her to slowly grow into that savings rate. Using the same inputs as before, just a 1% increase for those 14 years and a flat 15% savings rate from then until retirement would grow her balance to £1.4 million.

A 1% annual savings rate increase was worth more than £1 million over the life of Karen's portfolio.

Again, automate the process as much as you can. If, for example, you're given the option to increase your savings automatically each year without you having to think about it, then take it.

ACCEPT ANY HELP FROM YOUR EMPLOYER

Some employers will agree to pay more into your pension pot if you agree to increase your contributions to the scheme as well. This is known as 'contribution matching'. Effectively it's free money, so whatever you do, don't turn it down. Most employers will have a limit to the additional contributions that they will match. If you can't go up to the limit straightaway, you should aim to do so as soon as you can.

AVOID LIFESTYLE CREEP

The ability to witness your friends getting rich or buying stuff without getting jealous is a financial superpower. Lifestyle creep is one of the biggest deterrents to saving money because the more you make, the more you feel you deserve. Making more money can make your life easier, but you must ensure your spending rate doesn't outpace your savings if you ever wish to truly build wealth.

Let's go back to our 30-year-old saver, Karen. She still makes £60,000 a year and saves 2% of her salary. Her salary is increased by 3% each year by her employer. Now let's assume she makes no other changes than saving half of her annual raise every year, thus allowing her to spend the remaining half to improve her standard of living. I call this the save-plus-reward strategy. Saving half of her raise each year would nearly double Karen's balance on her 2% savings rate from £256k to £433k.

Now let's take this one step further and see what would happen if Karen saved half of each raise *and* increased her savings rate by 1% until it hit 15% by her mid-40s. Now by age 65 she has almost £1.6 million.

Starting small and slowly working your way up to your savings goal by avoiding lifestyle creep can provide a huge boost to your retirement savings.

TURBO CHARGE
YOUR INCOME

Saving money is important, but cutting back on your spending can only take you so far in life financially. Most financial experts preach the virtues of frugality to get ahead, but earning more money is how you supercharge your savings. The best investment you'll ever make is in yourself. Negotiating a £10,000 pay rise early in your career could be worth close to £1,000,000 over the course of your career. Here are three different scenarios that show what this single pay increase could turn into if you prioritise it in terms of saving:

	Save 25% of Annual Pay Rise	Save 50% of Annual Pay Rise	Save 75% of Annual Pay Rise
After 10 Years	£33,982	£67,965	£101,947
After 20 Years	£112,368	£224,737	£337,105
After 30 Years	£292,934	£585,867	£878,801

Assumptions: 6% annual return and 3% rise each year on an initial £10k rise in salary.

Now think about how much of an impact a few pay rises over the course of your career could have on your wealth if you approach them in this manner. You have to make a concerted effort to save any additional income, but the hard part for most people is actually earning more money.

There are whole books devoted to this subject. But there are two pieces of advice we would urge you to focus on.

HELP TO SOLVE YOUR BOSS'S PROBLEMS

Try to look at things from the perspective of your manager. Most bosses care more about making *their* lives easier than yours. So ask yourself: what are the problems they face and how can I help to solve them? What work do they do that they don't enjoy and that I can offer to do for them? Making your boss's life easier will put you at the front of the queue for a pay rise.

BECOME COMFORTABLE NEGOTIATING

Most people don't particularly enjoy negotiation – British people especially! But if you want to earn a higher salary you can't shy away from uncomfortable conversations. So, do your research, believe in yourself and be your own salesperson. Calmly and politely explain why you deserve to be paid more. It has nothing to do with arrogance; it's about demonstrating value that deserves to be rewarded.

Once you figure out how to get to that goal of a double-digit savings rate you need to figure out where to put that money.

CHAPTER 7.
WHAT TO INVEST IN

L ET'S SAY YOU want to start a new business. FastFish – the Uber of fish and chips – is aimed at people who want Britain's most famous dish delivered to their door within 15 minutes of frying. You think there'll be a big demand, but you don't have enough money to get your idea off the ground.

You have two options to turn your dream business into reality:

1. Option one is to borrow money from a bank through a small business loan where you pay back the principal over time with interest.

2. Option two is selling equity in the business to family, friends or outside investors where they are

entitled to a portion of the business' profits and the proceeds if the business is sold or goes public.

There are pros and cons to each funding option. If FastFish does wonderfully, there is huge potential upside for anyone who purchased an ownership stake to earn higher profits or see the value of their ownership stake increase. A lender, on the other hand, is only going to make the agreed upon interest income payment and get their principal repayment when the loan comes due.

If, on the other hand, FastFish does terribly, there is a huge potential downside for anyone who purchased an ownership stake to see lower profits and the value of their ownership stake fall or even going to zero in the worst-case scenario. A lender, on the other hand, is legally obligated to their debt repayments and would be first in line for any payments or asset forfeitures before the stockholders in the event of a bankruptcy – if people decide fish and chips on demand isn't something they're interested in.

Financial assets have a similar risk profile. Investing in stocks offers big potential upside but it comes at the risk of big downside potential. Owning high-quality debt or bonds lowers the risk of large losses but that protection is offset by the fact that your upside potential is capped. Cash flows paid to the owners of stocks are also far more volatile than those for bondholders because corporations have their own unique business risks and can get into trouble if the economy struggles.

There is no right or wrong answer in terms of how you deploy your capital between being an owner (stocks) and being a lender (bonds). But, how you allocate your money between the two is one of the most important decisions you will make as an investor because it sets the tone for your portfolio's risk profile.

If you only understand one concept about the risk of investing your capital, let it be this: you cannot earn high returns on your money over the long run without accepting losses or bone-crushing volatility at times. And you cannot keep your money safe from losses and bone-crushing volatility over the short run if you're not willing to accept lower returns over the long run.

Risk never goes away completely, it just gets transferred somewhere else. This is the essence of risk and reward when investing your savings.

Understanding risk and reward in the stock market is the subject of our next chapter.

CHAPTER 8. HOW THE STOCK MARKET WORKS

IT'S TIME TO talk again from personal experience. After getting engaged, Ben and his wife began having some deep philosophical conversations about how they would run their joint finances. They were in their mid to late 20s at the time and Ben informed her he would like to put the majority of their savings into the stock market.

This was obviously a topic initiated by Ben since he was the personal finance nerd of the relationship, but she was all for it. They discussed their spending habits, budgeting, saving, debt, bill payments and how they generally planned on setting long-term financial goals.

It was a great talk and one we recommend every couple have at some point if they plan on staying together for the long haul. The fastest way to lose half of your money is not through a stock market crash but in a divorce, so it's a good idea to make sure you're on the same page when it comes to your finances.

Since Ben and his wife both come from similar backgrounds in terms of saving, spending, credit card debt and living below their means, this was a pretty easy conversation considering how problematic finances can be for some couples. But there was one area where Ben's wife needed more clarity. And that was the topic of investing savings in the stock market.

Like many normal people, Ben's wife did not know much about the stock market except for what she heard on the news or saw on TV and in the movies. She did not give much thought to investing in stocks. So when Ben told her they would be saving the bulk of their money in stocks (especially when they were younger), she was initially concerned.

Aren't stocks extremely risky?

Isn't this just gambling with our money?

Isn't there a chance we could lose most of our money?

Shouldn't we just play it safe?

Working in the finance industry, Ben was no stranger to an Excel spreadsheet or PowerPoint presentation but he needed to put this explainer into plain English to avoid boring her and get his point across. What follows is more or less what he told her.

The stock market is the only place where anyone can invest in human ingenuity. It is a bet on the future being better than today. Stocks can be thought of as a way to ride the coattails of intelligent people and businesses as they continue to innovate and grow. Short of owning your own business, buying shares in the stock market is the simplest way to own a slice of the business world.

The greatest part about owning shares in the stock market is you can earn money by doing nothing more than holding onto them. When companies pay out dividends to shareholders, you get cold hard cash sent to your investment account which you can choose to either reinvest or spend as you please. The stock market is one of the few places on earth where you can earn passive income without having to do any work whatsoever. All you have to do is buy and wait. And if global stock markets don't go up over the long term, you'll have bigger problems on your hands than the size of your investment portfolio.

In short, risk and return in the stock market are related. That doesn't mean that taking risk guarantees a return; it doesn't. But you can't have one without the other. If there were no risk involved with owning shares, you would have no right to expect to be rewarded with healthy returns.

The bad news is, there's no way of telling whether now is a good time or a bad time to invest on the stock market. The good news is that for those with a long enough time horizon it really doesn't matter.

Many people compare the stock market to a casino, but in a casino the odds are stacked against you. The longer you play in a casino, the greater the odds you'll walk away a loser because the house wins based on pure probability. It's just the opposite in the stock market.

The longer your time horizon, historically, the better your odds are at seeing positive outcomes. Now these positive outcomes don't guarantee a specific rate of return, even over longer time frames. If the stock market were consistent in the returns it spits out, there would be no risk. But investors who are patient are almost always rewarded.

By way of example, the chart below shows the returns delivered by the S&P 500 index in the US since 1926. In any one year, there was a one-in-four chance of returns being negative. But there wasn't a single 20-year period which saw negative returns.

S&P 500: 1926–2020

Time Frame	Positive	Negative
Daily	56%	44%
1 Year	75%	25%
5 Years	88%	12%
10 Years	95%	5%
20 Years	100%	0%

Source: Dimensional Fund Advisors.

Returns, then, are nothing if not inconsistent, and average returns are actually very rare. As you can see from the next table, the best annualised (or average annual) return from the S&P 500 over a five-year period was 36.1%. The worst annualised return was a negative return of 17.4%. That's a huge difference. But the longer the time period, the smaller the gap between the best and worst returns.

S&P 500 Annual Returns: 1926–2020

	5 Years	10 Years	20 Years	30 Years
Best	36.10%	21.40%	18.30%	14.80%
Worst	-17.40%	-4.90%	1.90%	7.80%
Average	10.10%	10.40%	10.90%	11.20%

Source: Dimensional Fund Advisors.

So, it was possible to lose money over a ten-year period. Even over 20 years and 30 years, there was a big spread between the best and worst outcomes. However, even the worst annual returns over 30 years would have produced a total return of more than 850%. This is the beauty of compounding. The worst 30-year return for the S&P 500 gave you more than eight times your initial investment.

The stock market is a compounding machine in other ways as well. Since 1950, the largest companies in the US stock market have seen dividends paid out per share grow from roughly $1 to $60 by 2020. Profits have grown from $2 a share to $100 a share. Those are growth rates of roughly 6,000% and 5,000%, respectively, over the past 70 years or so, which is good enough for 6% annual growth for each. One dollar invested in the US stock market in 1950 would be worth more than $2,000 by the end of 2020.

$10,000 dollars invested in the S&P 500 in the year:

- 2010 would be worth $37,600 by September 2020

- 2000 would be worth $34,200 by September 2020

- 1990 would be worth $182,300 by September 2020

- 1980 would be worth $918,500 by September 2020

- 1970 would be worth $1,623,500 by September 2020

- 1960 would be worth $3,445,000 by September 2020

We're ignoring the effects of fees, taxes, trading costs, etc., here but the point remains that over the long haul, the stock market is unrivalled when it comes to growing money. The longer you're in it, the better your chances of compounding. And although the numbers differ from country to country, other major markets, including the UK, have performed in a not-dissimilar way.

Having said all of that, there is an unfortunate side effect of this long-term compounding machine. Stocks can rip your heart out over the short term. If there is an ironclad rule in the world of investing, it's that risk and reward are always and forever joined at the hip.

You can't expect to earn outsized gains if you don't expose yourself to the possibility of outsized losses. The reason that stocks earn higher returns than bonds or cash over time is because there will be periods of excruciating losses.

That $1 invested in 1950 would grow to $17 by the end of 1972 and subsequently drop to $10 by autumn of 1974. From there it would grow to $95 by the autumn of 1987, only to drop to $62 over the course of a single week because of the Black Monday crash. That $62 would have turned into an unbelievable $604 by spring of 2000. By the autumn of 2002 that $604 would have been down to just $340. After slowly working its way all the way to $708 by the autumn of 2007, over the next year and a half it would be cut in half down to $347 by March 2009. By the end of December 2009 that initial $1 was worth $537, which is less than the $590 it was worth a decade earlier at the end of 1999. So, $1 growing into $2,000 sounds amazing until you realise the many fluctuations it took to get there.

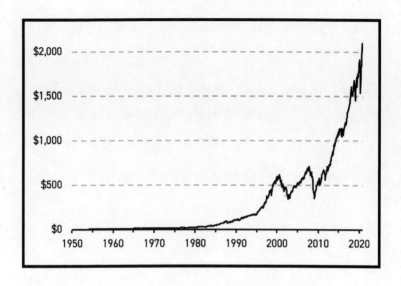

The stock market goes up a lot over the long term because sometimes it can go down by a lot over the short term.

The stock market is fuelled by differences in opinions, goals, time horizons and personalities over the short term, and fuelled by fundamentals over the long term. At times this means stocks overshoot to the upside and go higher than fundamentals would dictate. Other times stocks overshoot to the downside and go lower than fundamentals would dictate. The biggest reason for this is because people can lose their minds when they come together as a group. As long as markets are made up of human decisions it will always be like this. Think about how crazy fans can get when their team wins, loses or gets screwed over by the refs. These same emotions are at work when money is involved.

How you feel about investing in the stock market should have more to do with your place in the investor's lifecycle than your feelings about volatility.

Now let's look at the importance of lifecycle investing.

CHAPTER 9.
THE INVESTOR'S
LIFECYCLE

A S WE WRITE this book, Ben is feeling very sensitive about an imminent landmark birthday. Robin, meanwhile, would love to be 40 again so isn't as sympathetic as he might be. One thing we can agree on, though, is how quickly the years go by the older you become, so be sure to make the most of life whatever age you are.

Even in retirement, most people tend to have some exposure to the stock market. Depending on the actuarial charts you use, current life expectancy in Britain for someone in their mid-40s in 2020 is somewhere around 84 for men and 87 for women. So, if we live to that sort of age, both of us expect to be investing for several decades yet.

Realistically, Ben will be investing for another 40 years or more. In that time he's expecting to experience around ten more bear markets, about half of which will constitute a market crash in stocks. There will also probably be at least seven or eight recessions in that time as well.

Can he be sure of these numbers? You can never be sure of anything when it comes to the markets or economy, but let's use history as a rough guide on this.

Over the 50 years from 1970–2019, there were seven recessions, ten bear markets and four legitimate market crashes with losses in excess of 30% for the US stock market. Over the previous 50 years from 1920–1969, there were 11 recessions, 15 bear markets, and eight legitimate market crashes with losses in excess of 30% for the US stock market. The figures for European markets, including the UK, are fairly similar.

Bear markets, brutal market crashes and recessions are a fact of life as an investor. They are a feature, not a bug, of the system in which we save and invest our money. You may as well get used to dealing with them because they're not going away anytime soon. They can't go away, because the markets and economy are run by humans and humans always take everything, both good times and bad, too far.

The risk of these crashes and economic downturns is not the same for everyone though. How you view the inevitable setbacks when dealing with your life savings has more to do with your station in life than how scary you think those times are. Risk means different things to different people depending on where they reside in the investor's lifecycle.

When you're young, human capital (or lifetime earning potential) is a far greater asset than your investment capital. If you're in your 20s, 30s or even 40s you still have many years ahead of you as a net saver and earner, meaning market volatility should be welcomed, not feared.

There's an old saying that the stock market is the only business where the product goes on sale and all of the customers run out of the store. Your actions during down markets have a larger say in your success or failure as an investor than how you act during rising markets.

Down markets lead to higher dividend yields, lower valuations and more opportunities to buy stocks at lower price points. It may not feel like it at the time, but if you're saving money and putting it into the stock market regularly, more opportunities to buy stocks at lower price points is a good thing.

The problem is, during a market crash, it will always feel like it's too late to sell but too early to buy. If time is on your side, you shouldn't worry about nailing the timing of your investments, especially during down markets. The good thing about being a young person is you don't need to worry about timing the market to succeed. You have the ability to wait out bear markets since you have such a long runway in front of you. The important thing for you is to keep saving and investing regularly, no matter what is happening in the stock market.

People who are nearing the end of their working lives, on the other hand, are lacking in human capital, but they should, in theory, be sitting on plenty of financial capital. People are living longer, meaning the management of your money isn't over when you retire. But you have to be more thoughtful about how your life savings are invested at this stage of life because you don't have nearly as much time to wait out a down market, nor do you have the earning power to deploy new savings when stocks are down by buying when there's blood in the streets.

Market risk not only has different connotations depending on where you are in the investor's lifecycle, but also how your personality is wired. Your risk profile as an investor is determined by some combination of your ability, willingness and need to take risk. These three forces are rarely in a state of equilibrium so there will always have to be some trade-offs:

1. Your **ability to take risk** involves your time horizon, liquidity constraints, income profile and financial resources.

2. Your **willingness to take risk** involves your risk appetite. It's the difference between your desire to grow your wealth and your desire to protect your wealth.

3. Your **need to take risk** involves determining the required rate of return necessary to reach your goals.

Those who are unprepared for retirement may need to take more risk in their portfolio to achieve their goals, but they may not have the willingness or ability.

Those who have more than enough money saved may have the ability and willingness to take more risk to grow their wealth, but they may not need to because they have already won the game.

Rarely do the planets align when it comes to figuring out the right investment mix, but the good news is there is no such thing as the perfect portfolio. The perfect portfolio only exists with the benefit of hindsight. And even if the perfect investment strategy did exist, it would be useless if you couldn't stick with it over the long term. A half-decent investment strategy you can stick with is vastly superior to an extraordinary investment strategy you can't stick with. Discipline and a long time horizon are the big equalisers when it comes to financial success.

Your ability to withstand losses in the market and stay the course with your plan come hell or high water comes down to some combination of time horizon, risk profile, human capital, temperament and ego. If you don't understand yourself, your circumstances and your deficiencies when making decisions about money, it's impossible to truly gauge your tolerance for risk.

Next we're going to explain why picking stocks is harder than you think.

CHAPTER 10.
PICKING STOCKS
IS HARDER THAN
YOU THINK

G ENERAL ELECTRIC (GE) was the largest company in the US stock market in the year 2000. Not only was it the biggest company in the market, but it was nearly double the size of the second largest corporation, Exxon. From the start of the new century in 2000 through the autumn of 2020, GE shares were down 80%, including the reinvestment of all dividends. Retirees who kept the bulk of their retirement assets in the stock are in a world of pain. Nearly one-third of GE's company pension plan was invested in company shares as recently as 2016.

Yet GE is anything but an isolated case. US corporate history is littered with examples of once-great stocks like Enron, Lehman Brothers and WorldCom that similarly fell from grace. Researcher Geoffrey West analysed the longevity of publicly listed US companies since the mid-20th century and made the following discoveries:

- Nearly 29,000 companies traded on the US stock market from 1950 to 2009. By the end of that period, almost 80% had disappeared (through buyouts, mergers, bankruptcy, etc.).

- Fewer than 5% of companies in the stock market remained over rolling 30-year periods.

- The risk of a company dying did not depend on its age. The probability of a five-year-old company dying before it turns six was the same as that of a 50-year-old company failing to reach age 51.

- Larger companies were just as likely to die as smaller ones. Just 12% of firms listed on the Fortune 500 in 1955 survived.

- The estimated half-life of US publicly traded companies was 10.5, meaning half of all companies that went public in any given year were gone in 10.5 years.

But it's not just the US that has a large failure rate for big corporations. At the start of 2019, only 30 of the original 100 UK stocks that made up the FTSE 100 when it was launched 35 years earlier were still in the index.

The bad news, then, is that simply surviving as a corporation is hard enough. Over the long term, the vast majority of stocks underperform the broader stock market. The good news is that there's always a small number of hugely successful stocks that more than compensate – which brings us to the one question that people like Ben who work in the financial industry are asked more than any other.

What do you think of (such and such a company) I'm considering buying shares in?

There is typically a look of befuddlement on their faces when Ben politely declines to offer guidance with his standard, "I don't know."

The truth is he really doesn't know. And nor does Robin.

Why not? Because, contrary to popular opinion, picking stocks is fiendishly hard. In fact, our suggestion is that you don't even try.

One of the secrets to successful investing is that stock-picking isn't nearly as important as people in the financial media would have you believe.

Here's a shortlist of things that are *more* important:

- **Your savings rate.** Saving is the first step to investing.

- **Your asset allocation.** The mix of shares, bonds, cash and other investments will be the biggest determinant of your investment success beyond how much you save because it sets the tone for the risk profile of your portfolio.

- **Your investment plan.** Financial writer Nick Murray says, "A portfolio is not, in and of itself, a plan. And a portfolio that isn't in service to a plan is just a form of speculation; it can have no other goal than to beat most other people's portfolios. But 'outperformance' isn't a financial goal."

If a portfolio isn't a plan then neither is stock-picking. We'll admit, picking stocks is more fun than asset allocation, but it's also much harder to pull off. For every Amazon that turns a small initial investment into millions of pounds, there are thousands of companies that would decimate your life savings.

An eye-opening study from JP Morgan found roughly 40% of all stocks in the US stock market have suffered a permanent 70%+ decline from their peak value since 1980. Two-thirds of all stocks underperformed the stock market itself in that time, while 40% of companies experienced negative returns.

There have, of course, been some big winners in this time, but it is a select group of stocks. Around 7% of companies in the US stock market have generated lifetime returns that would put them in the category of 'extreme winners'. According to Hendrik Bessembinder's research, four out of every seven stocks in the United States has underperformed the return of cash sitting in a savings account since 1926. There are simply more opportunities to pick the losers than the winners in the stock market.

And remember, there's losing and there's losing big. If you buy an individual share, it could go to zero. In other words, you could lose your entire investment.

The answer, then, is simple: *diversify*. Don't focus on individual stocks; seek exposure to whole markets. Don't pick out one or two sectors of the economy; have a stake in every major sector. Don't just invest in the UK or the US stock market; be a truly global investor.

Instead of looking for needles in a haystack, just buy the whole haystack.

Or, to use a cricketing analogy, stop trying to hit a six off every ball. You simply need to stay in the game. So be happy to accept ones and twos, carefully avoiding rash investments that could decimate your life savings.

In short, forget getting rich quick and focus on getting rich slowly. How to go about it is the subject of our next chapter.

CHAPTER 11.
THE ONE-STOP SHOP
INVESTMENT FUND

MOST OF US are familiar with fantasy sports teams. Ben knows a bit about NFL, and every year he's asked by friends, neighbours or co-workers to join a fantasy team. Robin is a longstanding football (or, as Ben calls it, soccer) fan and receives similar invitations at the start of every Premier League season. But we both politely decline to take part. Nothing against those who are into made-up sports teams, but it's just not for us.

In fact, our feelings about fantasy sport are similar to the way many people feel about their investment portfolios. Some people simply don't have the energy or inclination to keep tabs on how all the different components are performing. Nor do they want the hassle of picking funds or shifting their risk exposure as their circumstances change. And there's nothing wrong at all with this line of thinking.

Of course, you could if you wanted have more control. Some hobbyist investors find investing intellectually stimulating and are happy to put in the time and effort required to construct their custom investment portfolio. For the majority of people though, there are two solutions which will make their investing lives very much easier.

In this chapter we're going to focus on the first of those solutions – target-date funds, sometimes known as TDFs.

Target-date funds are a relatively new innovation in the UK and are one of the best developments for individual investors in decades.

Why?

Because they take many of the investment decisions out of your hands and automate the process for you. It's a huge step forward for normal investors who don't have the bandwidth to do this themselves.

So how do target-date funds work?

Each target-date fund has a literal date in its name that signifies when you would be retiring. So, let's assume you're 35 years old and plan to retire at age 65. If you started investing in the year 2021, a target date 2051 fund would line up with your time horizon since the retirement date on that fund is 30 years away.

These all-in-one funds invest across asset classes (stocks and bonds) and regions of the world to give you a well-diversified portfolio. The investment company that manages the fund chooses the asset allocation based on your age, shifting from a stock-heavy portfolio in your younger years into a more balanced allocation as you near retirement. This change to the portfolio mix is called the glide path because it's a gradual shift over time. The investment company will also automatically rebalance the fund for you back to the stated asset class target weights over time.

Target-date holdings can vary by fund company, but if you want to take more or less risk depending on your appetite for stocks, you can always choose a fund with a different retirement date. For instance, let's assume Patrick is 25 but is still unsure of his ability to deal with losses in the stock market. Instead of going with a target date 2060 fund, he could pick the 2050 or 2045 option which would have a lower allocation to stocks. Or how about Paula, who is 45 but plans on working well into her 70s and is willing to accept more stock market risk. Instead of going with the 2040 target-date fund, she could pick the 2050 or 2055 fund to hold more stocks.

Most UK company pension schemes now offer either target-date funds or so-called 'lifestyle' funds. There are subtle differences between the two, but TDFs and lifestyle funds have similar objectives and both are sensible options. TDFs are increasingly becoming the default investment choice when employees join a new workplace pension scheme.

You can also invest in a target-date fund or lifestyle fund in a Stocks and Shares ISA. The major investment platforms will all offer access to these funds.

Target-date funds aren't perfect. You can't customise the holdings to suit your exact needs or asset allocation preferences. There's no one there to hold your hand or explain exactly how these funds work (retirement advice varies by plan sponsor and is often severely lacking). The allocations and glide paths can vary depending on the fund company. As with all investment strategies you could do better, but it's also much easier to do worse than a target-date fund. If nothing else, TDFs are an excellent way for investors who are just starting out to gain exposure to a broadly diversified portfolio without having to work out the specific holdings themselves.

If you want a greater degree of customisation, you can always sign up with an online investment provider, known as a robo-adviser. Again, robo-advisers aren't perfect. For a start, despite their name, most of them don't actually provide advice. But they do allow you to create a portfolio just for you that suits your specific needs and goals. Perhaps the best feature of these services is the fact that the saving and investing is automated for you after you sign up and fill out some general information about your circumstances.

The beauty of using an all-in-one fund or an automated investment solution is that it cuts down on the temptation to tinker with your portfolio. They're designed to protect you from your worst impulses as an investor and can reduce the temptation to make poor investment decisions at the worst possible time.

So, we mentioned there are two solutions for those who don't want the bother of designing and monitoring an investment strategy. Target-date funds are the first. We're about to introduce you to the second – indexing.

CHAPTER 12.
YOU GET WHAT YOU DON'T PAY FOR

AS EVERY CONSUMER knows, you generally get what you pay for. The more you pay for something, whether it's a meal out, a holiday or a washing machine, the better you expect it to be in terms of quality. The Skoda Fabia or Dacia Sandero are both perfectly good cars, but there's a reason why you can buy at least ten of those for a new Aston Martin Vantage.

But what if we told you that, with investing, the opposite is true? That the less you pay to an investment provider, the better your outcome is likely to be? Well, that's exactly how it is.

As we've already explained, picking stocks that will outperform the stock market is extremely difficult. Why? Because the stock market is very efficient. Current share prices reflect all known information about a particular company and so how are you going to find novel, unknown information about a company that the rest of the market does not know as well? It's very hard to do. The theory behind this is called the efficient market hypothesis (EMH).

Instead of trying to pick winning investments in individual companies, Ben and I recommend investing in index funds, or trackers, which hold every single company in a particular market. Instead of paying for an *active* fund manager to choose stocks for you, or instead of trying to choose individual company investments yourself, index investors choose to invest *passively* in the whole market. That market might be the FTSE 100 of the 100 biggest UK companies, the whole UK market of all UK companies, or indeed the whole global market of all companies listed on stock markets worldwide.

Now, you can argue the toss about just how efficient markets are, but it's fair to say that they're efficient enough to be very hard to beat. Studies have shown that, over the long term, only a tiny fraction of actively managed funds succeed in beating the market.

And what's more, those very few funds are almost impossible to identify in advance.

There is however a more fundamental reason for using passive funds over active ones – they're much cheaper.

It was the late Jack Bogle who launched the first index fund available to ordinary investors, the Vanguard S&P 500 Index Fund, in the mid-1970s. Instead of EMH, Bogle liked to refer to CMH, the cost matters hypothesis:

> The case for indexing isn't based on the efficient market hypothesis. It's based on the simple arithmetic of the cost matters hypothesis. In many areas of the market, there will be a loser for every winner so, on average, investors will get the return of that market less fees.

Index funds are hard to beat because you get to keep more of the returns by paying lower fees than investors pay in actively managed funds. Not only are the expenses lower on these funds, thus offering you a larger percentage of the take-home return, but they trade less, meaning there are fewer transaction costs. This idea of the cheaper product being better is the exact opposite of most things you buy in other areas of your life, which is one of the reasons investing can be so counter-intuitive.

Investment research firm Morningstar performed a study that looked at all of the variables that predicted the future success or failure of a mutual fund in terms of its performance. The variable with the higher predictive power had nothing to do with the intelligence of the portfolio manager selecting the stocks or their ability to forecast the future or which university they attended. The variable with the most predictive power was cost. Looking across every asset class, Morningstar found the cheapest 20% of funds were three times more likely to succeed than the most expensive 20% of funds.

When it comes to investing, being cheap is a virtue.

If you based your investment decisions on nothing other than choosing the funds with the lowest costs, you would likely do better than 70–80% of all investors. All else equal, if you're choosing a fund for your company pension or investment account, picking the one with the lowest cost is a good starting point. And if you're picking a target-date fund, try to find the one that holds mostly index funds. Holding low-cost funds doesn't guarantee that you'll earn higher returns on your savings, but it does guarantee you'll take home more on a net basis than the alternative, the majority of the time.

Compound interest can provide a tailwind over the long haul when it comes to growing your wealth, but fund fees can quietly counteract this advantage if you're not careful.

So, whether you're using a target-date fund or a robo-adviser, ensure that your investments are passively managed and low-cost. As a rule of thumb, you should only consider a fund with an annual management charge of less than 0.30%.

The cheapest investments tend to be exchange-traded funds, or ETFs. But beware: not all ETFs are passively managed. Do your research and read the small print before signing up.

And once you've built your portfolio and set up automatic monthly payments into your pension or investment account, here's what we recommend you do: *nothing*. That's right, the less you do, the less you think about it and the less you check your account balance, the better your returns are likely to be.

As the famous investor Benjamin Graham once wrote, "The investor's chief problem – even his worst enemy – is likely to be himself."

In the next chapter, we're going to show you a simple and highly effective way to stop you meddling with your investments.

CHAPTER 13.
DIVERSIFYING
ACROSS TIME

O NE OF THE biggest benefits the advent of
target-date funds has provided to individual
investors is the ability to diversify their investments in a
simple, cost-effective manner using a single fund. But
there is another simple way to diversify your investing
that has nothing to do with the investments you choose.

Murphy's Law states anything that can go wrong
will go wrong. Investors often feel this way about
the timing of their purchases into the stock market.
There's always a nagging worry that you'll invest your
money right before a huge crash. The beauty of being
a long-term investor is that your purchases are spread
out over a wide range of market environments.

The majority of normal investors aren't investing on day one with a huge pool of capital unless they have uber-rich parents or a large inheritance. Instead, you're investing money periodically out of your salary or making contributions on a set schedule from your bank account, slowly but surely building your wealth.

This is known as pound-cost averaging.

It's diversifying across time, because sometimes you're buying when markets are screaming higher, sometimes you're buying when markets are getting crushed, and sometimes you're buying when markets are somewhere in-between. If you're investing consistently like this, it means sometimes you'll buy more shares with the same amount of money (when markets are falling) and sometimes you'll buy fewer shares with the same amount of money (when markets are rising).

The most important aspect of pound-cost averaging is that you simply keep buying no matter what.

Trying to get too cute with the timing of your purchases is sure to lead to suboptimal results eventually, because market timing is a game no one can win consistently. This is true even if you try to create a strategy where you only buy when markets are down, which seems counterintuitive to the oldest investment advice in the world – buy low and sell high.

Financial writer Nick Maggiulli performed a study to test this theory by comparing two buying strategies – one simple and one *God-like*. The first strategy would invest £100 (adjusted for inflation) into the US stock market every month for 40 years. We'll call this the simple approach to investing. The God-like strategy was completely unrealistic but it assumes you only put that £100 to work at the absolute low point between two all-time highs in the market. So this isn't just a buy low strategy, but a buy at the bottom of the market in every cycle strategy.

So which approach was the winner?

Shockingly, the simple approach beat God, scoring a 70% win rate going all the way back to the 1920s. And missing the exact bottom of the market in the God-like strategy would take the win rate for that strategy from 30% to just 3%. Plus, no one is good enough to buy at or near the bottom of every bear market. This example shows the tortoise beating the hare even when the hare has Usain Bolt's speed. Maggiulli concludes, "Even God couldn't beat pound-cost averaging."

The reason the simple approach beats God is because investing on a regular basis over the long haul gives your savings more time to grow. Constantly trying to invest at the bottom of the market means sitting on the sidelines and missing out on valuable dividend payments and market appreciation. And since the stock market, over time, goes up more often than it goes down, you could be waiting a long time for a better entry point if you try to time your purchases.

When pound-cost averaging, sometimes you buy higher. Sometimes you buy lower. Sometimes you buy when stocks are undervalued. Sometimes you buy when stocks are overvalued. The only thing that matters is that you keep buying. You're not beholden to any single point in time.

When viewed from this perspective, volatility in the stock market is no longer your enemy but your friend. It allows you to average in at different price points during different market environments. As a net saver, you should welcome down markets from time to time. Young people with decades ahead of them should say a prayer for falling markets every night before they go to bed.

The only thing that matters is that you keep buying. Fortunately, when you invest part of your salary automatically each month by direct debit, this is already happening.

All of this is especially true when stocks go down – and we can assure you they will.

CHAPTER 14.
STOCKS WILL
GO DOWN

OVER THE LONG term, the stock market is a good place to be. Between 1900 and 2020, the annualised real return on US equities was 6.6%; the global figure, excluding the US, was 4.5%. The annualised real return on UK equities was 5.4%.

That's not bad, especially when you consider all the challenges the global economy faced in that time – two world wars, Communist revolutions in Russia and China, the threat of nuclear holocaust and the rise of global terrorism among them. Whatever else you might think about capitalism, it has proved remarkably resilient.

There is, however, a *but*, and it's this: although the long-term trajectory of markets was upwards, there were frequent occasions when the patience of equity investors was sorely tested. Along with death and taxes, stock market declines are an unavoidable part of life.

Market downturns, when they happen, can be stomach-churning. Take the crash of March 2020, for example. Markets began falling in the last week of February on fears about the spread of coronavirus. There was another steep decline on 9th March. Two days later, President Trump announced a travel ban from Europe and, on 12th March, the Dow Jones Industrial Average fell 9.99%. It soon became clear that a recession was inevitable and, on 16th March, the DJIA dropped another 12.93%, or 2,997 points – the largest point drop since Black Monday in 1987.

We now know, with the benefit of hindsight, that the panic would be short-lived. The Nasdaq surpassed its pre-crash high in June 2020, followed by the S&P 500 in August and the Dow in November. But for anyone with significant exposure to the stock market these were scary times.

Since 1950, the US stock market has been the world's top performer. Yet, in that time, even US equities have experienced double-digit losses in more than half of all years. Nine out of every ten years has seen losses of at least 5% at some point during the year. So it's perfectly normal for markets to freak out on a periodic basis, because humans freak out from time to time as reality does not always line up with expectations.

As an investor in the stock market, you have to get used to existing in a state of loss because the market is below all-time highs the majority of the time. Since 1928, the S&P 500 has hit new all-time highs in roughly 5% of all trading sessions. If we invert this number, that means 95% of the time investors are in a state of drawdown and stocks are down from a previous high watermark.

In the short term, the reasons for market sell-offs feel like they matter a lot and downturns feel like they'll never end. In the long term, investors tend to forget the specific reasons stocks fell in the past and all corrections look like buying opportunities.

Another benefit of making periodic contributions to your investment account is the psychological boost this can provide in the midst of a downturn. This is especially true for those just starting out on their retirement savings journey without a sizeable portfolio just yet. An investor who doesn't have a lot of money set aside should be able to withstand

larger percentage losses because the actual decline
in pounds will be relatively small. On the other hand,
an investor with a lot of money in their portfolio can
see a relatively small percentage loss lead to a much
bigger loss in terms of pounds. For example, these are
the losses in pounds based on different portfolio sizes
and percentage losses:

Loss	£10,000	£50,000	£100,000
-10%	(£1,000)	(£5,000)	(£10,000)
-20%	(£2,000)	(£10,000)	(£20,000)
-30%	(£3,000)	(£15,000)	(£30,000)
-40%	(£4,000)	(£20,000)	(£40,000)
-50%	(£5,000)	(£25,000)	(£50,000)

Loss	£250,000	£500,000	£1,000,000
-10%	(£25,000)	(£50,000)	(£100,000)
-20%	(£50,000)	(£100,000)	(£200,000)
-30%	(£75,000)	(£150,000)	(£300,000)
-40%	(£100,000)	(£200,000)	(£400,000)
-50%	(£125,000)	(£250,000)	(£500,000)

As Captain Obvious likes to say, "The bigger your
portfolio the more money you lose for a given
percentage decline." This works in both directions, as
the inverse of these losses would show greater gains
with larger portfolio balances as well.

When you have a small portfolio that you're looking to make into a big portfolio, you have the ability to make up for short-term losses by increasing your savings rate. We can call this your savings replacement rate. Let's assume you invest £500 a month, or £6,000 per year. These are the savings replacement rates for various loss levels based on these same portfolio sizes.

Losses covered if contributing £6,000 per year

Loss	£10,000	£50,000	£100,000
-10%	600%	120%	60%
-20%	300%	60%	30%
-30%	200%	40%	20%
-40%	150%	30%	15%
-50%	120%	24%	12%

Loss	£250,000	£500,000	£1,000,000
-10%	24%	12%	6%
-20%	12%	6%	3%
-30%	8%	4%	2%
-40%	6%	3%	2%
-50%	5%	2%	1%

A 20% downturn on a £25,000 portfolio would lead to losses of £5,000. It's never fun to see that money temporarily disappear, but investing £6,000 in that year would more than make up for the market value loss and leave you with an ending balance of £26,000.

Captain Obvious here again – making regular contributions and sticking with it doesn't improve your performance, but it could help you stay the course during a market downturn if you're still able to see some progress. Here are those same results if you maxed out your Stocks and Shares ISA, which has a max contribution limit of £20,000 in the 2021–2022 tax year.

Losses covered if contributing £20,000 per year

Loss	£10,000	£50,000	£100,000
-10%	2000%	400%	200%
-20%	1000%	200%	100%
-30%	667%	133%	67%
-40%	500%	100%	50%
-50%	400%	80%	40%

Loss	£250,000	£500,000	£1,000,000
-10%	80%	40%	20%
-20%	40%	20%	10%
-30%	27%	13%	7%
-40%	20%	10%	5%
-50%	16%	8%	4%

If you have £250,000 saved in your ISA, a 20% loss would mean £50,000 has evaporated for the time being. That stings, but maxing out your ISA would cover 40% of those losses.

It's also worth pointing out losses in the overall stock market aren't permanent. The only permanent losses during a panic come when you sell.

This line of thinking is more about optics than anything, but psychological tricks can come in handy during down markets because behaviour is the first thing to go during stressful market situations. Sometimes you have to fool yourself into staying the course because the temptation to sell is so great when prices are all over the map.

Tricking yourself into saving more can be more useful than most people imagine because knowledge alone is never enough to change your behaviour.

CHAPTER 15.
WHEN INFORMATION
IS USELESS

CONSIDER THE FOLLOWING:

- In the 1960s only between 1% and 2% of adults in England were obese.

- By 2019 the number was 28%.

- A further 36% are overweight but not obese.

- Obesity is the second leading cause of preventable death.

The biggest head-scratcher of these numbers is the fact that the diet and exercise craze really took off for the first time in the 1960s. People spend more money on this stuff than ever before, yet the results are going in the wrong direction. There are no official statistics on how much we spend on diet products, but the UK diet industry is said to be worth an estimated £2 billion a year. Spending on gym membership and exercise equipment has also grown. However much money we throw at this problem, it seems to get worse.

Human nature is such a powerful force that it can act against your own best interests. Knowledge alone is never enough to change behaviour.

Statistics don't stick with us but stories do. Most people prefer get-rich-quick schemes to thoughtful advice on how to get rich slowly for the same reason people seek out fad diets. Tactics are easier to latch onto than wholesale lifestyle changes because they make you feel like you're accomplishing something. This is the opposite of the power of small wins. It's the acceleration of small losses.

It is a cliche at this point to compare personal finance to dieting and fitness, but this is as good of an explanation as any as to why financial literacy fails to help people improve their money skills. The solutions for both personal finance and getting healthy are fairly simple in theory:

- For your finances: spend less than you earn, live below your means, prioritise your spending, save and invest early and often, and don't take on excessive levels of debt.

- For your health: exercise regularly, don't overindulge, avoid too much sugar and carbs, eat less, and plan your meals in advance.

Unfortunately, this information is useless unless it's paired with an intelligent concrete plan to change behaviour. It's estimated that 95% of people who lose weight using a diet end up gaining the weight back. Bad habits are hard to break.

Food researcher Brian Wansink once wrote, "The best diet is the one you don't know you're on."

This is a wonderful way to think about implementing a workable saving and budgeting plan as well. Automating your saving and spending is up next.

CHAPTER 16.
TREAT YOUR SAVINGS LIKE A NETFLIX SUBSCRIPTION

CARTOONIST RANDY GLASBERGEN drew a single-frame cartoon that perfectly encapsulates the conflict that occupies nearly every financial decision you make in life. It depicts a man sitting in his financial adviser's office saying, "Explain to me again why enjoying life when I retire is more important than enjoying life now."

This is deep.

This inner struggle can be taken to both extremes. There are those people who save nothing, live from payday to payday and never plan ahead for their future financial well-being. And then there are those people who are frugal to a fault and never spend any money or enjoy themselves. For the rest of us, we are constantly trying to strike a balance between enjoying life now and ensuring we have the resources to enjoy life later.

There is no ideal balance for everyone because we all have different goals, needs, resources, expectations, and desires. The hardest part about planning for your financial future is the simple fact that no one knows what's going to happen. No one has it all figured out because no one knows the curveballs that life is going to throw at them.

It's fair to say, for both of us, that our thoughts have changed over the years. We've both been savers for as long as we can remember. So, balance for us has been reminding ourselves that it's OK to spend money on those areas we care about and cut back on everything else. A life with a full bank account but no experiences or enjoyment is pointless. But a life with an empty bank account can steal your enjoyment now and also later in life, so there are always trade-offs to consider.

You can find information about markets and investing just about everywhere these days. Personal finance advice is now as abundant as it's ever been, but the focus is typically on ways to save money. Saving is obviously important but the other side of the equation doesn't get nearly enough attention – spending money. No one ever teaches you about how to spend – or more importantly, how to prioritise how you spend.

One of the reasons this is the case is because no one actually enjoys budgeting, since the concept generally makes people feel bad about themselves. Yet understanding how and where you spend your money is perhaps one of the most important aspects of a successful financial savings plan.

There are generally two approaches to budgeting:

1. **Manual.** Track every single item you spend money on down to the last penny to understand where your money goes.

2. **Autopilot.** Automate as much of your spending and saving as humanly possible and spend whatever is left over.

The manual option is for those who require a full overhaul of their financial ecosystem and do not want to utilise technology in their financial plan. Personal finance guru Dave Ramsey recommends an envelope-based system where you put all of your cash into different spending categories. Those envelopes could be labelled groceries, clothes, entertainment, petrol, etc. And when the money runs out of one envelope, either you're done spending in that category or have to pull from another category. The envelope system is essentially used to control how much you spend in each area of your life.

There is nothing wrong with the manual approach, but we prefer the autopilot version because it requires less ongoing maintenance. Putting your finances on autopilot requires more work up front but the benefits can last a lifetime.

Putting your finances on autopilot requires setting up the following tasks:

- Automatic bill paying for every periodic expense.

- Automatic credit card payments to avoid crippling debt, high interest payments, and late fees.

- Automatic investment contributions to your ISA or pension.

- Automatic debt repayments.

The more you can take these decisions out of your own hands the better, because it helps cut down on unnecessary late fees and overdraft charges on your bank account. It's estimated the biggest credit card companies make roughly $100 billion a year on late fees and interest charges alone. If you have your accounts on autopilot you don't have to worry about those types of unnecessary charges because every month your credit card will be paid off automatically.

And once you become a true personal finance ninja, you can pay for all of your automatic charges with a credit card that offers rewards so the large financial institutions are actually paying you to use their services. These rewards can come in the form of travel points, cash back and even contributions to investment or savings accounts. The fact that these companies are able to offer rewards to cardholders shows you how much money they make off borrowers who don't pay off their bills on time.

'Pay yourself first' is one of the oldest personal finance rules in the book for a reason – it works. Willpower is fleeting so if your strategy is to save whatever is left over every month, you're bound to come up short eventually. Most people simply spend what's available until there are no leftovers.

The trick is to treat your savings like a Netflix subscription that gets paid every month on a set schedule.

Work out how much you're going to invest in your ISA or pension plan each month and simply set up a direct debit for that amount. With workplace pensions, you're generally asked to select a set percentage of your salary as your monthly contribution, and it's automatically deducted from your salary. Effectively, the money's invested on your behalf automatically before you're ever tempted to spend it. This is crucial because inertia is one of the biggest enemies of behavioural change.

If you don't set these systems up in advance it becomes harder to do so later after you become comfortable with your current level of pay. In countries where the default approach to organ transplants is that people are automatically signed up until they actively choose to opt out, 90% of people register to donate their organs. In countries where the default approach is to exclude people from the programme unless they choose to sign up on their own, the rate of people registering is just 15%. Defaults are very powerful.

The fund management company Vanguard conducted a comprehensive study of the workplace retirement plans it runs in the US. It found that firms which offered an automatic enrolment system with an opt-out saw savings rates that were 56% higher than firms which asked employees to opt in. It also found that employees under the age of 35 who make less than $50,000 a year had a savings rate that was twice as high when their employer used automatic enrolment instead of voluntary enrolment in their retirement plan.

Automating as much of your financial ecosystem as possible frees you up to spend less time on your finances. You simply spend whatever is left over after your investment savings and bills have been auto-deducted from your bank account. This allows you to spend money without feeling guilty about it because you've already taken care of the financial necessities. It also forces you to spend more on those things that make you happy and cut back elsewhere. Of course, this strategy still requires some thought about what spending areas truly matter to you. But getting to a point where you're more aware of your priorities can help identify those places where you can cut back on spending to ensure there's less waste in your financial life.

Whichever route you choose, there are enormous benefits to understanding your spending habits because it helps you understand where your priorities lie.

If you can't get your priorities in line, it will be impossible to build your long-term investments in any meaningful way and get closer to financial freedom.

CHAPTER 17.
ENLIST THE HELP
OF THE TAXMAN

WE'VE EMPHASISED THE importance of keeping your costs to a minimum and, at risk of boring you, here's another reminder:

> The less you pay to invest, the more money you keep for yourself.

It really is that simple.

But there's one cost of investing that people tend to overlook, and that's tax.

If you're a UK citizen and you make a profit when you sell shares or other assets such as Bitcoin, you may have to pay Capital Gains Tax. You will need to make a note of any gains you make, declare them on your tax return and pay any tax owing.

The good news is that, if you're smart about it, you shouldn't need to pay any tax at all, regardless of the size of the gains you make. Better still, savvy investors actually enlist the help of HMRC and get the taxman to make substantial contributions to their long-term investments.

The best investment strategies are usually the simplest. So, our suggestion is that you confine your savings and investments to as few accounts as possible.

Do bear in mind that the rules regarding tax on savings and investments are subject to change, so be sure to check the latest information. But, at the time of publication, your best option for your emergency fund is a Cash ISA. Using an ISA, any interest you earn will be tax-free.

Once your emergency fund is in place, you need to be investing in equities, which have of course delivered far higher returns historically than cash.

As things stand at the time of going to print, the best starting point for young investors is a Lifetime ISA, or LISA. As long as you didn't turn 40 on or before 6 April 2017, you are eligible to have one.

Here's the deal. For every £4 you invest, the government will add £1 – a benefit worth up to £1,000 every tax year until you turn 50. This 25% bonus is payable on the first £4,000 you invest and it's paid every month.

The only catch with a LISA is that if you take any money out before the age of 60 and spend it on anything other than your first house, you'll be hit with a 25% penalty when you withdraw your cash. In other words, the government wants to incentivise you to invest for the long term which, as we've explained, it is in your interests to do.

But, if you do want the flexibility to take your money out and spend it on what you want, you should invest in a third type of ISA, known as a Stocks and Shares ISA, alongside your Cash ISA and LISA.

Regardless of how many ISAs you have, the maximum you're able to invest in any one year is £20,000.

If you like the idea of the taxman contributing to your savings and investments, we haven't told you the half of it. That's because the government is even more generous when it comes to pensions. There are even more generous tax incentives on offer here.

When paying into your pension, you receive tax relief on any contributions that you make. This is at the highest rate of income tax that you pay, provided that the total gross pension contributions you make do not exceed your annual earnings or what's called the annual allowance, which is capped at £40,000.

In other words, if you're a 20% taxpayer, the taxman puts in an extra 20 pence for every pound you invest. If you pay tax at 40%, the government contributes 40 pence for every pound.

For your pension investing, you can either choose to make additional contributions to your workplace pension, or set up a personal pension and contribute to that. You will get the tax relief in either case.

Think about it. Why risk your money on a trading platform, when you can invest, via your pension, in index funds that spread your risk between every stock on a particular market – and when the government will chip in with an extra 20% or 40% of tax relief.

So, why share a chunk of your investment returns with HMRC when you don't actually need to? Instead of paying the taxman, get the taxman to pay you. Invest as much as you reasonably can in a combination of ISAs, plus a workplace pension or personal pension.

With all of this saving and investing that we are recommending, when, realistically, will you become financially independent? We'll take a look at that in the next chapter.

CHAPTER 18.
WHEN WILL I
HIT FINANCIAL
FREEDOM?

WHEN YOU FIRST set out to save and invest, you might be stuck on the idea of becoming rich. As you age and priorities shift, that mindset often turns into a fear of dying poor.

Do I have enough money saved?

What if the market crashes just as I quit work?

What if I need long-term care?

How can I be sure my money will last?

These are all legitimate questions worth considering, but this goes to show you the uncertainties around financial independence. Stock market crashes and recessions can be scary to live through, especially for those who have given up work and are no longer earning money with their human capital. Your biggest risk is not market or economic volatility, but running out of money.

Managing your finances for financial independence requires a balance between the need for stability in the short term versus the need for growth in the long term. Even a 2% inflation rate would nearly cut your purchasing power in half over 30 years if you simply buried your money in the garden. Most investors will be forced to take some risk and accept some volatility in their portfolio to ensure they have enough money to see them through the long haul.

The behavioural psychologist Daniel Kahneman once asked, "How do you understand memory? You don't study memory. You study forgetting." This is how to think about the problem of figuring out how much money you need for financial independence as well.

How do you understand how much you need for financial independence? You don't figure out a number. You figure out how much you spend and save. It's pointless to try to figure out how much you'll need in savings or income if you don't have a good understanding of how much it costs for you to live.

Where you are in your lifecycle will obviously have a lot to do with how you think about these factors. In your younger years, it's almost impossible to plan ahead for the exact amount you'll need based on the exact amount you'll spend later. There are simply too many variables to consider, many of which can and will change over a period of years.

As you get older, you'll have a much better grasp of how much you spend on an annual basis and what your wants, needs and desires will be later in life. From those numbers, you can come up with a better estimate to determine how much of a nest egg you'll need to cover your annual expenditures from your portfolio.

You'll never be able to work out how large your portfolio will need to be if you don't have a deep understanding of your spending. Your monthly burn rate is a pretty good starting point when thinking through how far your savings will take you. And it's not only the things you spend your money on that matter but the things you don't spend your money on.

Is your mortgage paid off? Do you have any other outstanding consumer debt? Are your kids off your payroll? The combination of a high savings rate going into financial independence along with a dearth of debt obligations can make your savings last much longer than the alternative. Going into financial independence with little in the way of debt increases your financial flexibility enormously. High fixed costs are your biggest enemy when seeking financial independence.

Investing when you're older does introduce some new variables and risks to the equation you have to be aware of. Getting a handle on your spending helps, but you still have to figure out how much to take from your portfolio each year, which investments to take from and which accounts offer the most tax-efficient withdrawal strategy.

Financial markets never move in a straight line so this process requires some flexibility depending on how things shake out in the markets and how your spending evolves later in your life.

Your investment plan doesn't need to change every time stocks rise or fall, but you do have to incorporate real-world market performance with your built-in expectations. Any useful investment plan takes into account the need for course corrections on occasion.

As the old saying goes, "Plans are useless but planning is indispensable."

It will be nearly impossible to implement a sound investment plan if you don't have a handle on your sources of income once you've stopped working. For some people this could simply include their state pension, once they're old enough, and investment income from their portfolio. Others could have a pension plan, an inheritance, rental income from a second home, or a part-time job to supplement their spending needs.

There are all sorts of risks to consider later in life, including outliving your money, inflation, emergencies, unplanned one-time expenses, healthcare costs, the sequence of your investment returns and general market volatility. This is why diversification among stocks, bonds, cash and other assets is so important. It helps you plan for the wide range of outcomes life tends to throw at you.

All of this can seem overwhelming, but the first step in the process boils down to figuring out what you want to do with your life once you've stopped working. You'll never be able to figure out your finances if you don't first figure out what you want to buy with your life savings. The entire reason you're saving in the first place is to purchase your freedom. You're buying your own time.

So what are you going to do with that time? Travel? Volunteer? Read more? Spend more time with family? Only work on projects that interest you? People often spend decades investing their money without giving a second thought to how they'll invest their time. Studies have shown that experiences and giving back to others often bring the greatest happiness and help ward off the potential depression which can afflict many who leave the working world.

You can run through all the calculations and spreadsheets you want, but life will inevitably get in the way as some of your assumptions will be proven wrong. This is an unfortunate side effect of trying to plan in the face of irreducible uncertainty. In a way, there's a lot of guessing involved in the process. This is why financial planning is a process and not an event. You don't simply set a course of action and follow that exact plan forever. Financial plans should be open-ended because there will always be corrective actions, updates, changes in strategy and difficult decisions that have to be made.

There's never a perfect time to say, "I'm financially independent," just like there's no such thing as a perfect portfolio. If you have your personal finances in order, understand how much it costs you to live, where your income will be coming from once you've stopped working and how you'll spend your days, that's a pretty good start.

But what if you want to ensure you'll become a millionaire? Up next is a look at what's required.

CHAPTER 19.
HOW TO BECOME
A MILLIONAIRE

WHEN BEN AND Robin were growing up, £1 million seemed like a huge sum of money. But because of inflation, that's the kind of sum you might need in the not-too-distant future to reach financial freedom.

There's nothing special about the million pound mark per se but it's a wealth threshold people have held in high esteem ever since novelist and future prime minister, Benjamin Disraeli, first used the term 'millionaire' in the 1820s.

How feasible is it to become a millionaire? Let's take a look at the numbers. Say you invest the current

ISA limit of £20,000 a year, these are the investment returns required to reach £1 million by the age of 65:

Starting Age	Required Return For £1 Million at Age 65
30	2%
35	3%
40	5%
45	8%
50	13%

Assumes £20,000 invested annually.

If you've been following along throughout the book, it's not a ground-breaking discovery to point out how helpful it is to begin saving at a young age. The required return to hit £1 million for someone who saves £20,000 a year in their 30s is a relatively low hurdle. Wait to start saving until you're in your late 40s or 50s and it's much harder to get to seven figures because your required rate of return is higher.

Obviously, saving £20,000 each year is not an easy task, especially in your 30s. Student loans, a mortgage deposit, kids and everything else life throws at you means few people have the means to max out their retirement savings at that stage in life.

It's also tough to go from 0 to 60 and save £20,000 a year without slowly building up to that level. Few individuals or households have the means to go to that level of savings straight out of the gate.

Let's say you want to take advantage of the power of small wins by slowly increasing the amount you save over time until that max contribution level is hit.

If you were to begin saving at age 30 at the following monthly amounts and increase those contributions by £100 a month each year until you reach the maximum, these are the corresponding required returns:

Initial Monthly Savings	Initial Annual Savings	Required Returns
£250	£3,000	3.3%
£350	£4,200	3.1%
£450	£5,400	2.9%
£550	£6,600	2.7%
£650	£7,800	2.5%

Assumes you increase contributions by £1,200 a year (£100 a month) until you're putting in £20,000 a year.

Start at age 30 and stop at age 65.

Here's the same exercise starting at age 35:

Initial Monthly Savings	Initial Annual Savings	Required Returns
£250	£3,000	5.1%
£350	£4,200	4.7%
£450	£5,400	4.4%
£550	£6,600	4.2%
£650	£7,800	4.0%

Assumes you increase contributions by £1,200 a year (£100 a month) until you're putting in £20,000 a year.

Start at age 35 and stop at age 65.

And once more using age 40 as the starting point:

Initial Monthly Savings	Initial Annual Savings	Required Returns
£350	£4,200	7.4%
£450	£5,400	6.9%
£550	£6,600	6.5%
£650	£7,800	6.2%
£750	£9,000	5.9%

Assumes you increase contributions by £1,200 a year (£100 a month) until you're putting in £20,000 a year.

Start at age 40 and stop at age 65.

The required returns are surprisingly low in these examples, but everything looks easier on paper than in real life, especially when money is involved. Saving, investing and getting your personal finances in order are always more of an exercise in psychology than maths. It would be irrational of me to suggest that everyone should be able to become an investing millionaire because some families or individuals are simply never going to be able to save this much money on a regular basis.

Whether you become a millionaire or not, there are some lessons from this data:

CONSISTENCY MATTERS BUT LIFE IS INCONSISTENT

Consistently saving money from a relatively young age over time can make up for a lack of investment acumen or lower than average returns from financial markets. But consistently saving money in a linear fashion over time is probably one of the hardest things to do because life is inconsistent. If you're a robot, saving up a large nest egg should be an easy feat. Unfortunately, you're not a robot and it's not easy. Life is full of curveballs. Plan accordingly.

CHANGE CAN DISRUPT YOUR INVESTING PLANS

The only way numbers like this work is if you never stop making contributions. Turning a little money into a lot of money is about patience, but patience is useless without a side serving of discipline and consistency.

'ENOUGH' MEANS DIFFERENT THINGS TO DIFFERENT PEOPLE

There is no perfect number when it comes to saving and investing. The end goal will always depend on your circumstances, standard of living, spending preferences, lifestyle choices and relationship with money.

———

Most of the saving exercises in this book are meant to drive home the benefits of saving from a young age, but all is not lost if you got a late start on saving and investing.

In the next chapter, we'll look at what you need to do if you waited to get started with investing until your 40s or 50s.

CHAPTER 20.
WHAT IF YOU GET
A LATE START
INVESTING?

THERE ARE MANY reasons so many people in the older age bracket have a lack of savings and investments. Some people simply don't make enough money to set aside enough for their later years. Others have bad luck in their career, horrible financial role models, poor personal finance habits or a lack of knowledge when it comes to money management. Both Ben and Robin have children and they can understand why many parents would put their children first when it comes to their spending priorities.

Whatever the reason, there are a number of people who wish they had started saving when they were younger but didn't. Beginning the process of saving and investing in your 40s or 50s isn't ideal but it's not a lost cause either. If you made a late start there are still steps you can take to build up your investments. You just have to make some potentially uncomfortable moves and stop wasting time. The best time to start saving was ten years ago, but the second best time is today. Don't be discouraged if you're in this place. Many people in this same situation give up, saying it's too late, but that's not the case.

Older savers may have some potential advantages. You should be in your peak earnings years. Hopefully the kids are out of the house and off your payroll. Empty-nesters could use the money they were using to fund their children's university or other costs and funnel them into savings. The same is true if you get to the point where you pay off your mortgage. If you've already been making those debt repayments for many years, you can immediately shift those payments to your savings.

You might be tempted to shoot for the moon and take on tons of risk with your investments to play catch-up, but saving money is still far more important than how you invest when we're talking a period of maybe

10–20 years to build up your investment balance before retiring.

Let's assume Carl and Carla Carlson are both 50 years old with little in the way of investments and savings. The kids are now out of the house so they can supercharge their savings to make up for lost ground. Carl wants to take more risk to make up for their shortfall while Carla would rather increase their savings rate to make up for lost ground.

The Carlsons currently have a household income of £100,000 that will grow at a 2% cost of living adjustment each year. Carla expects their investments to compound at 6% annually and would like to save 20% of their income, while Carl thinks he can do much better than that by trading stocks and saving a little less. Carla thinks Carl is too overconfident in his stock-picking abilities and would rather save more money than take on a riskier investment strategy.

The couple wants to retire by age 65 or 70 but are unsure how far their savings can get them in such a short amount of time. Let's look at an example which shows their current plan, one with a higher savings rate and one where Carl's stock picks knock it out of the park:

Savings Rate	Investment Return	After 10 Years	After 15 Years	After 20 Years
10%	6%	£143,977	£264,029	£432,112
20%	6%	£287,954	£528,058	£864,225
10%	12%	£192,013	£418,634	£826,370

Assumes £100k income growing at 2% per year.

Even if Carl did come up trumps with his trading account and doubled up Carla's 6% return target, a higher savings rate would have still led to better results. A doubling of the Carlsons' savings rate from 10% to 20% led to a better outcome than a doubling of their investment returns from 6% to 12%, even over a two-decade period. And chances are Carl is not the next Warren Buffett, so increasing their savings rate is far easier than increasing their investment returns.

Taking more risk in your portfolio doesn't guarantee you anything in the markets. The market won't give you good returns just because you need them. Your savings rate is something you control while no one controls the returns thrown off by the financial markets. A more likely scenario is by taking more risk Carl would actually harm the performance of their savings because the track record of professional, let alone amateur, stock-pickers is so poor.

Saving at an early age is important because it helps you build solid financial habits and allows compound interest to snowball your money over time. But saving is probably even more important for those who are behind on their retirement savings because you don't have as long to allow compounding to do its thing.

Now this doesn't mean your time horizon as an investor is done right when you retire. According to the Office for National Statistics, a couple retiring today have more than a 50% chance that at least one of them will live into their 90s. You could still have two to three decades to manage your money during your post-work years. It's just that your time as an earner and saver may have a shelf life if you don't work during retirement.

There are other ways for Carl and Carla to extend the life of their portfolio. A simple solution is to delay their retirement. Investment expert Charles Ellis found that delaying your retirement from age 62 to age 70 could reduce your required savings rate by more than 50%. If you don't like the idea of working full-time when you're 70, part-time employment is a possible compromise.

Most people would prefer not to work beyond their mid-60s, but for those who are willing and able it can drastically increase your odds of success in retirement.

It not only means you can save more money but also allows your money to compound for longer.

Working for longer has other benefits too. A US study published in 2020 found that people who work beyond the age of retirement were "healthier, less isolated, and happier" than those who don't. The researchers also pointed out that "work provides opportunities for learning, reasoning, and social engagement, all of which help stave off the adverse effects ageing can have on the brain." They cited a long-term study into the memory function of more than 3,000 British civil servants over a 30-year period, covering the final part of their careers, as well as the early years of their retirement. The study showed that verbal memory, which declines naturally with age, deteriorated 38% faster after retirement.

In summary, having to play catch-up to fund life after work is an unenviable position to be in. But if that's where you are, don't despair. You do still have options. Just stop making excuses and get your act together. Running out of money in your later years is no fun for anyone.

Up next – financial advice. Can you manage without an adviser? Or do the benefits outweigh the cost of paying for one?

CHAPTER 21.
DO YOU NEED
A FINANCIAL
ADVISER?

THIS IS A self-help book. We wanted to keep it simple and concise. Of course, there's plenty more reading you could do, but we've told you pretty much everything you really need to know about investing and the steps towards achieving financial freedom.

Something you might be wondering is, now we've shown you the ropes, whether you need a financial adviser.

The simple answer, for many people, is no. The priority for young investors is simply to get started. You also need to develop good habits, to control your spending and to invest what you can every month in a low-cost index fund. You don't really need an adviser for any of those things.

There are several online investment providers to choose from that will get you up and running and give you the option to automate your contributions. Research the options carefully. You're looking for a solution that's transparent and inexpensive, and which primarily uses passive funds.

Increasingly, the new "robo-adviser" investment providers offer access to a real-life financial adviser, usually via video conferencing. For those who prefer to speak to a fellow human being when making important decisions (and that, let's face it, is most of us) this hybrid approach is an excellent option.

What we would say, though, is that there comes a point in life when most people would benefit from having a financial adviser – someone who understands them and knows their financial situation in detail, and whom they can turn to whenever they need to.

Research by Vanguard has shown that a good adviser can add about 3% to your net investment returns every year. Over the course of your investing lifetime, that can add up to a substantial sum.

How does a financial adviser add this value? It's not, as many people seem to think, through special insight into the financial markets or the prospects for the global economy. Advisers have no more idea than you do about where the markets are headed in the short to medium term.

Nor do they know which are the best shares, funds, countries or asset classes to invest in at any particular time, although many advisers like to give the impression they do. The evidence shows, overwhelmingly, that no one can predict the market with any consistency. You don't want to pay thousands of pounds a year for a fortune teller. You can buy a crystal ball on Amazon for less than a tenner.

No, an adviser adds value by setting a suitable asset allocation, keeping control of your costs and, most of all, through behavioural coaching. As we've explained, it's best for young investors if markets fall when they're starting out. That way they're buying shares at a lower price. But as your portfolio grows, it can become harder to hold your nerve in turbulent markets. An adviser can help you keep a level head.

By persuading their clients not to bail out of equities during a correction, or not to go all-in when markets seem to be heading inexorably higher, advisers can easily repay their fees several times over.

If you don't want to pay for an adviser, we would certainly encourage you to identify someone to act as a sounding board. It may be a friend or family member, but it needs to be someone you can trust. You're not asking them to offer advice, but simply to listen to your rationale for any big financial decision you make. Rather than someone who will simply reaffirm your thinking, choose someone who is likely to challenge you, to ask you questions and to point out something you may have overlooked.

Another important point to remember is that helping to improve investment outcomes is just one of the services a financial adviser provides. The best firms are able to help you with anything to do with your finances, or at least point you towards someone else who can. That might be choosing the right mortgage or an appropriate level of insurance; it might be tax planning or passing on your wealth to the next generation.

In our view, though, there is something that definitely is worth paying for at some stage, and that's holistic financial planning, or financial life planning as it's sometimes called.

Some advisers focus entirely on money. But money is only a means to an end, and without wanting to sound overly philosophical, the end is to live a life of contentment and fulfilment. A holistic financial planner can help you to connect money with meaning – to use your money in a way that reflects your goals and values.

Strange as it may seem, many people don't give serious thought to what they really want. They go through life without even knowing what their goals and values actually are. In many cases, they've held self-limiting beliefs from childhood about the things that really matter to them and the role that money plays in their lives. Having a financial planner who can challenge those beliefs is extremely valuable.

We're assuming that most people who read this book are attracted to the idea of financial freedom. But financial freedom means different things to different people. Sooner or later you're going to need to decide what it is you want to do with that freedom, so that, at the end of your life, you don't have any regrets.

Again, it might be there's a friend or relative you can trust to help you work this out, to help you write a one-page plan and periodically check, in the years ahead, that you're continuing to stick to it. But, one day, we would certainly encourage you to consider hiring a holistic financial planner on an ongoing basis.

A final word on finding an adviser. The right adviser is well worth paying for. But a poor adviser can do more harm than good. Do your research carefully and ask the right questions. Here are some examples:

Do you have an evidence-based investment philosophy?

Do you understand the value of behavioural coaching?

Do you offer cashflow modelling so I can see for myself that I can afford the lifestyle I want?

Do you provide proper, holistic financial planning or just advice on investments?

Another important consideration, as you would expect, is cost. Most advisers in the UK charge a percentage of the client's investible assets. That tends to work to benefit those with smaller portfolios, but as your wealth grows it can work out very expensive. So, it's worth considering a firm with a fixed-fee model instead, or one that charges by the hour.

Ultimately, choosing the right adviser all boils down to trust. Ask yourself, can I really trust this person?

Can I be sure that they genuinely have my very best interests at heart?

Trust is, of course, a very personal and subjective issue. Only you can make that call. But, if you get it right, it might turn out to be one of the best decisions you will ever make.

CHAPTER 22.
THE 20 RULES
OF PERSONAL
FINANCE

PICTURE YOURSELF GETTING ready for a family
summer road trip.

You have an itinerary all laid out for every stop along
the way including the hotels you'll stay at, the sites
you'll see and you've checked the Google reviews for
the various restaurants you plan to eat at on your trip.

The day finally arrives when you plan to depart. The
anticipation for a trip is often more exciting than the
vacation itself, so your entire family is hyped up and
ready to go.

Everyone piles into the family car, ready to go, until someone realises Dad forgot to fill up with petrol, no one packed their suitcases, someone forgot to bring the snacks and there isn't a single iPad on board to keep the kids happy in the backseat.

The finance equivalent here is coming up with the world's greatest investment strategy without first realising the importance of personal financial planning. Yes, investing is important if you would like to compound your wealth over time, but it doesn't matter if you can't save money and get your financial house in order first.

Here are 20 basic rules to put you on a sound financial footing:

1. **Avoid credit card debt like the plague.** The first rule of personal finance is never carry a credit card balance. Credit card borrowing rates are egregiously high and paying those rates is an easy way to negatively compound your net worth. Not all debt is necessarily bad, but credit card debt is by far the worst. If you have credit card debt, you're not ready to invest your money in the markets.

2. **Building credit is important.** The biggest expense over your lifetime will probably be interest costs on your mortgage, car loans and student loans.

Having a solid credit score can save you tens or even hundreds of thousands of pounds by lowering your borrowing costs. Use credit cards to build a solid credit history by always paying off the balance each month. Putting all of your automated bills on a card that's automatically paid off each month is a good place to start.

3. **Income is not the same as savings.** There is a huge difference between making a lot of money and becoming wealthy, because your net worth is more important than how much money you make. It's amazing how many people don't realise this simple truth. Having a high income does not automatically make you rich; having a low income does not automatically make you poor. All that matters is how much of your income you set aside, not how much you spend. Anyone can spend money to appear wealthy, but true wealth comes from the absence of spending in the form of saving.

4. **Saving is more important than investing.** Pay yourself first is such simple advice, but so few people do this. The best investment decision you can make is setting a high savings rate because it gives you a huge margin of safety in life. You have no control over the level of interest rates, stock market

performance or the timing of recessions and bear markets, but you can control your savings rate.

5. **Live below your means, not within your means.** The only way to get ahead financially is to consistently stay behind your own earnings power. Living within or above your means is how you end up going from paycheck to paycheck without ever truly building wealth. The only way to get ahead is by living below your means and setting aside a portion of your income for the future. Delayed gratification is poor branding so just think about this in terms of the time you can buy yourself in the future to do what you want, when you want to do it.

6. **If you want to understand your priorities look at where you spend money each month.** You have to understand your spending habits if you ever wish to gain control of your finances. The goal is to spend money on things that are important to you but cut back everywhere else. And if you pay yourself first you don't have to worry about budgeting, you just spend whatever's left over on the things that truly matter to you.

7. **Automate everything.** The best way to save more, avoid late fees, and make your life easier is to automate as much of your financial life as

possible. The goal is to make the big decisions up front so you don't need to waste so much time and energy tending to your finances. If the bulk of your family's financial life is on autopilot, it should only take you an hour or so each month to keep track of everything.

8. **Get the big purchases right.** Do you really need a house with four or five bedrooms? Or a top-of-the-range four-by-four if most of your journeys are to and from your place of work? Personal finance experts love to debate the minutiae of shop-bought sandwiches and lattes, but the most important purchases in terms of keeping your finances in order will be the big ones – housing and cars. Overextending yourself on these two purchases can be a killer because they represent fixed costs and come with more ancillary expenses than most people realise.

9. **Build up your liquid savings account.** Your monthly spending levels should take into account the fact that there are infrequent, yet predictable, expenses you'll need to take care of on occasion. Weddings, holidays, car repairs and health scares never occur on a set schedule, but you can plan on paying for these events by setting aside small

amounts of money each month to better prepare yourself when life inevitably gets in the way.

10. **Cover your insurable needs.** This is another personal finance margin of safety item. Some people have too much insurance and others too little. Focus on the biggest risks that you and your loved ones face. Most importantly, consider the impact on your business or family if you were to die or become disabled. The idea is to measure that impact in pounds, and if possible, insure against it. Just remember that insurance is about protecting wealth, not building it.

11. **Take full advantage of employer contributions.** Again, it's important to pay as much into your pension as you reasonably can. But this is especially important for those in company schemes where the employer agrees to match the amount the employee puts in. Ideally you should aim to invest the maximum amount that your company is willing to match. Failing to do so is like turning down a pay rise. No one in their right mind does that.

12. **Save a little more each year.** Our suggestion is that you aim to save between 10% to 20% of your income. The trick is to increase your savings rate every time you receive a pay rise so you'll never

even notice you had more money to begin with. Avoiding lifestyle creep can be difficult, but that's how you build wealth. And the sooner you begin setting money aside, the less you end up realising it never made it to your bank account to be spent in the first place.

13. **Choose your friends, neighbourhood and spouse wisely.** Robert Cialdini has written extensively on the concept of social proof and how we mirror the actions of others to gain acceptance. Trying to keep up with spendthrift friends or neighbours is a never-ending game with no true winners. Find people to spend your life with who have similar money views as you and it will save you a lot of unnecessary stress, envy and wasteful spending. Don't worry about keeping up with the Joneses as much as following your own path.

14. **Talk about money more often.** It takes all of five minutes before people start talking about politics in almost any conversation these days, but somehow money is still a taboo subject. Talk to your spouse about money. Ask others for help. Don't allow financial problems to linger and get worse. Money is a topic that impacts almost every aspect of your life in some way. It's too important to ignore and sweep under the carpet.

15. **Material purchases won't make you happier in the long run.** There is something of a short-term dopamine hit we get through retail therapy, but it wears off. Buying stuff won't make you happier or wealthier because true wealth is all of the stuff you don't waste money on. Experiences give you a better bang for your buck and time spent with the people you love is one of the best investments you can make.

16. **Read a book or ten.** There are countless personal finance books out there. If it bores you to death then at least skim through a few and pick out the best pieces of advice from a few different sources to test out. This stuff should be taught in every secondary school and college, but it isn't. So you have to take the initiative. No one is going to care more about your money decisions than you. Invest some money, time, and energy into yourself. It's the best investment you can make.

17. **Know where you stand.** Everyone should have a back-of-the-envelope idea of their true net worth. Before knowing where you want to go you have to know where you are. That means adding up all of your assets and subtracting any debts. This way you can set some general expectations about savings rates, market returns and portfolio growth

to give yourself some goalposts in the future. Since reality doesn't always sync up with expectations, this allows you to make course corrections along the way to your savings rate, investment strategy or financial plan.

18. **Taxes matter.** Tax issues can be maddeningly complicated, but it's important to have a basic grasp of how the system works. The most important thing is to use accounts that allow you to save and invest free of tax. Also take advantage of tax relief on your pension contributions. As long as you're willing not to have access to it until you stop working, this is effectively free money going begging.

19. **Make more money.** Saving and/or cutting back is a great way to get ahead, but it's an incomplete strategy if you're not trying to earn more by enhancing your career. Too many people are stuck in the mindset that there's nothing they can do to get a better job, take on more responsibilities or earn higher pay. You must learn how to sell yourself, improve your skills and negotiate a higher income over time. A £10,000 pay rise could be worth hundreds of thousands of pounds over the course of your career.

20. **The goal is financial independence.** The goal shouldn't be about making it to a certain age so you can ride off into the sunset, but rather getting to the point where you don't have to worry about money any more. Time is the most important asset in the world because you can't manufacture more of it. Becoming financially independent allows you to make decisions about how you spend your time on your own terms.

CONCLUSION: KEEP IT SIMPLE

I N THE 1840S a Hungarian physician named Ignaz Semmelweis noticed a large discrepancy in mortality rates for new mothers during childbirth in the two maternity wards in his hospital. While working at a hospital in Vienna, Semmelweis realised the doctors' maternity ward had three times the mortality rate of the babies being delivered in the midwives' maternity ward.

The biggest difference between the two wards was how the two groups of hospital workers spent their downtime. You see, the doctors and medical students experimented on cadavers in the morgue. The midwives did not. After working on the dead bodies, the doctors and students didn't wash their hands, thus transferred all sorts of germs to the new mothers during childbirth.

Semmelweis's recommendation to have the doctors begin washing their hands was initially ridiculed by the medical community because this flew in the face of established opinions held at the time. Germ theory had been proposed in the 19th century but many experts still believed in the spontaneous generation of germs and bacteria.

Obviously, Semmelweis was proven right eventually, but it took time for people to change their minds. The life expectancy for new mothers rose dramatically. There is now a greater proportion of 20-year-old Americans who have a living grandmother than had a living mother in the year 1900.

It's amazing how something as simple as washing your hands can lead to such a vast improvement in the quality of life. This is a good reminder that advice doesn't have to be complicated to be effective.

The investing industry loves complexity, and so does the financial media. Investors are bombarded with new information and new ideas on where best to deploy their money. Around the world, the coronavirus lockdown saw a boom in amateur trading, particularly among young people. Technological advances have enabled us to trade whenever we want – and not just shares and bonds, but cryptocurrencies such as Bitcoin and complex financial instruments that are far riskier than many people trading them realise.

In some ways, of course, it's a positive thing that access to the financial markets is opening up. But it's fraught with danger too. Part of the problem is that we usually hear about success stories – people who've made a killing by betting on a small number of stocks and then offer courses to other traders to explain their 'system'. We rarely hear about the majority of traders who've either lost money or at least underperformed a simple low-cost index tracker.

It's human nature to think there must be a clever way to outperform other traders and investors systematically, if only we could discover what it is.

The fact is, however beguiling they find all this complexity to be, investors would be much better off looking for simplicity. Here are some of the reasons why:

- **It's easier to be fooled by randomness and complexity.** If you torture the data long enough it's bound to tell you exactly what you want to hear. Complexity invites data-mining, over-optimisation and seeing correlation where there is no causation.

Right or wrong, simplifying makes it harder to game your own system.

- **Complexity is about tactics; simplicity is about systems.** Tactics come and go, but an overarching philosophy about the way the world works can help you make better decisions in many different scenarios. Simple doesn't go out of style.

- **Simple is harder.** You have to fight to keep things simple because our natural human impulses make us susceptible to stories and narratives. Simplicity is more of a psychological exercise, while complexity is more about trying to outsmart the competition.

- **Complexity can lead to unanticipated consequences.** Simplicity has been described as the art of thoughtful reduction. Sherlock Holmes once said, "If you eliminate the impossible, whatever remains, however improbable, must be the truth." Complexity, on the other hand, opens you up to far more possibilities and surprises, and not always in a good way.

- **Complexity can give you an illusion of control.** As a coping mechanism, people look to avoid stress by giving themselves the illusion of control. Certainty makes us feel more comfortable, but really it's an illusion. Investors seek out a feeling of certainty and control, even if it means being wrong. Simplifying is about focusing on what you can control and understanding what you cannot.

- **Complex problems don't require complex solutions.** It's difficult to get people to buy into simplicity because it's hard to believe that complex problems don't require complex solutions. We all want to believe that the Holy Grail of investment sophistication exists and, if we can only find the secret sauce, all of our problems will be solved. This is why get-rich-quick schemes will always find an audience.

- **Simple is easier to understand.** It's hard to put a value on the ability to understand exactly what you're doing and why. Simplicity allows for more transparency. It's easier to set reasonable expectations. Charlie Munger once said, "Simplicity has a way of improving performance through enabling us to better understand what we are doing."

Get the basics right and you're 95% of the way to being a successful investor. Everything else will only make small differences around the edges.

If nothing else, make sure you do these three things:

1. Save a double-digit percentage of your income. There are no guarantees in life or finances but saving a decent chunk of your income is one way to allow some room for error. If you can't get to this goal right away, slowly increase your savings rate over time so you can see some small wins and work up to it.

2. Automate as much as humanly possible. Automate your bill payments. Automate savings from your paycheck or checking account. Automatically increase your savings rate every year. And make your investment strategy as rules-based as possible.

3. Get out of your own way. This is the hardest one for most people. Knowledge alone is not enough to change your ingrained human nature or the lesser version of yourself. Do the basic things described in this book and don't be tempted to meddle with them.

Could you do better by implementing a more complex approach to saving and investing? Possibly. There are people who have done so and succeeded. But you have better things to do with your time. Projects to work on. Spending time with your kids. Having dinner or drinks with friends. Creating a new business. Watching Netflix. You don't want to spend all of your time debating the minutiae of investment approaches and personal finance.

It's impossible to give blanket financial advice because so much of it boils down to circumstance, personality, station in life and your relationship with money.

However, if you can find a way to save 10% to 20% of your income into the financial markets each year, automate your savings, investments and bill payments, increase the amount you save each year by just a little, diversify your investments, and basically leave them alone, you needn't worry. You'll be much better off financially later in life than the vast majority of people. Everything else is gravy.

Amazon founder Jeff Bezos once asked Warren Buffett, "Your investment thesis is so simple, you're the second richest guy in the world, and it's so simple. Why doesn't everyone just copy you?"

To which Buffett replied, "Because nobody wants to get rich slow."

Getting rich slowly is far more realistic than getting rich quickly. No, it isn't easy. It also requires plenty of willpower, discipline and patience. But it's perfectly achievable if you know how to go about it.

These are some of the books that have had the biggest impact on our own personal finances over the years:

I Will Teach You To Be Rich by Ramit Sethi

The Millionaire Next Door by Thomas Stanley and William Danko

The Little Book of Common Sense Investing by Jack Bogle

Smarter Investing by Tim Hale

Your Money and Your Brain by Jason Zweig

Winning the Loser's Game by Charles D. Ellis

The Psychology of Money by Morgan Housel

Millionaire Teacher by Andrew Hallam

Wealth Management by Jason Butler

Own It! by Iona Bain

ABOUT THE
AUTHORS

Ben Carlson is the Director of Institutional Asset Management at Ritholtz Wealth Management in New York City. Ben has spent his career working with various nonprofits, institutions and families to help them plan and invest their money wisely. He is the author of three other books including *A Wealth of Common Sense: Why Simplicity Trumps Complexity in Any Investment Plan*, the co-host of the Animal Spirits podcast and author of the blog, A Wealth of Common Sense.

Robin Powell is a journalist and broadcaster and the editor of the investing and personal finance blog, The Evidence-Based Investor. He is Head of Client Education at RockWealth, an evidence-based financial planning network with offices across the UK. He also campaigns for greater fairness and transparency in the global asset management industry.

REFERENCES

INTRODUCTION

The Algebra of Wealth. profgalloway.com. Scott Galloway. 2021.

"How are younger generations faring compared to their parents and grandparents?" Jonathan Cribb. Institute for Fiscal Studies. 2019.

Earnings Outlook. Resolution Foundation. 2021.

"Inherited wealth on course to be a much more important determinant of lifetime resources for today's young than it was for previous generations." Pascale Bourquin, Robert Joyce and David Sturrock. Institute for Fiscal Studies. 2021.

Millennial Money Survey. Foreign & Colonial Investment Trust. 2021.

CHAPTER 1

The Fifties. David Halberstam. Open Road Media. 2012.

CHAPTER 2

The Power of Habit: Why We Do What We Do in Life and Business. Charles Duhigg. Random House. 2012.

Atomic Habits: An Easy & Proven Way to Build Good Habits & Break Bad Ones. James Clear. Penguin Publishing Group. 2018.

"Temporal Reframing and Savings: A Field Experiment." Hal E. Hershfield, Stephen Shu and Shlomo Benartzi. UCLA. 2018.

CHAPTER 3

"Retirement Success: A Surprising Look into the Factors that Drive Positive Outcomes." David M. Blanchett and Jason E. Grantz. *The ASPPA Journal*. 2011.

CHAPTER 4

"The History of the Air Jordan." Foot Locker www.footlocker.com/history-of-air-jordan.html

CHAPTER 5

The Investor's Manifesto. William Bernstein. Wiley. 2009.

CHAPTER 6

"Theo Epstein." The Axe Files. January 2017.

CHAPTER 10

"Beyond GE – US workers own too much company stock in retirement plans." Mark Miller. Reuters. July 2018. www.reuters.com/article/us-column-miller-employerstock/column-beyond-ge-u-s-workers-own-too-much-company-stock-in-retirement-plans-idUSKBN1K234Z

Scale: The Universal Laws of Growth, Innovation, Sustainability, and the Pace of Life in Organisms, Cities, Economies, and Companies. Geoffrey West. Penguin Publishing Group. 2017.

"The Agony & The Ecstasy: The Risks and Rewards of a Concentrated Portfolio, Eye on the Market Special Edition." Michael Cembalest www.chase.com/content /dam/privatebanking/en/mobile/documents/eotm/ eotm_2014_09_02_agonyescstasy.pdf

"Do Stocks Outperform Treasury Bills?" Hendrik Bessembinder. *Journal of Financial Economics*. 2018. papers.ssrn.com/sol3/papers.cfm?abstract_id=2900447

CHAPTER 12

"Fund Fees Predict Future Success or Failure." Russel Kinnel. Morningstar. May 2016. www.morningstar. com/articles/752485/fund-fees-predict-future-success-or-failure

"Even God Couldn't Beat Dollar Cost Averaging." Of Dollars and Data. Nick Maggiulli. February 2019. ofdollarsanddata.com/even-god-couldnt-beat-dollar-cost-averaging

CHAPTER 14

Credit Suisse Global Investment Returns Yearbook 2021. www.credit-suisse.com/about-us/en/ reports-research /csri.html

CHAPTER 15

The Dorito Effect: The Surprising New Truth About Food and Flavor. Mark Schatzker. Simon & Schuster. 2015.

Mindless Eating: Why We Eat More Than We Think. Brian Wansink. Bantam. 2007.

Health Survey for England 2019: digital.nhs.uk/data-and-information/publications/statistical/health-survey-for-england/2019

CHAPTER 16

"Opt Out Policies Increase Organ Donation." Francesca Scheiber. Stanford University. sparq.stanford.edu/solutions/opt-out-policies-increase-organ-donation

"How America Saves 2020." Brian Alling, Jeffrey Clark and David Stinnett. Vanguard. 2020. institutional.vanguard.com/ngiam/assets/pdf/has/how-america-saves-report-2020.pdf

"The Invisible Coach." Michael Lewis. Against the Rules. 2020.

CHAPTER 17

"These Workers are Saving the Maximum in Their 401(k) Plans." Darla Mercado. CNBC. August 2019. www.cnbc.com/2019/08/01/these-workers-are-saving-the-maximum-in-their-401k-plans.html

CHAPTER 18

"Fidelity Announces Q1 2018 Retirement Data: Saving Rates Hit Record High and Account Balances Continue to Increase Over Long-Term." Fidelity. May 2018. newsroom.fidelity.com/press-releases/news-details/2018/Fidelity-Announces-Q1-2018-Retirement-Data-Saving-Rates-Hit-Record-High-and-Account-Balances-Continue-to-Increase-Over-Long-Term/default.aspx

CHAPTER 20

Falling Short: The Coming Retirement Crisis and What to Do About It. Charles Ellis. Oxford University Press. 2014.

Working Longer Solves (Almost) Everything: The Correlation Between Employment, Social Engagement and Longevity. Tim Driver and Amanda Henshon. Wharton Pension Research Council Working Papers. 2020.

Effect of retirement on cognitive function: the Whitehall II cohort study. Baowen Xue et al. *European Journal of Epidemiology.* 2018.

CHAPTER 21

Quantifying Vanguard Advisor's Alpha. The Vanguard Group. 2019.

CONCLUSION

Fewer, Richer, Greener. Laurence Siegel. Wiley. 2019.